Born to Fly
A WOP/AG's War.

———

The wartime experiences of

Leslie Bruce Smith

By

Alan James Barker and Raymond Warrender.

With Foreword

by

Gary Mitchell.

Published by

Cauliay Publishing & Distribution
PO Box 12076
Aberdeen
AB16 9AL
www.cauliaybooks.com

First edition

ISBN 978-0-9568810-3-8
Copyright © Alan James Barker and Raymond Warrender

FOREWORD

I first got to know Leslie as a family friend over many years. As I am a serving aircrewman on a search and rescue helicopter unit based in Holland Leslie was always interested in my work. I clearly remember one question which Leslie asked was, "Did I ever get scared?" We got to know each other even better when it became clear that Leslie was also an aircrewman, or to be precise, a wireless operator / air gunner in Bomber Command and the Pathfinder Force during WW2. His flying and mine are in different categories yet the dangers of flying are one we share together. I was privileged to hear some of the experiences Leslie had endured after being called into service during Europe's darkest days. His survival in a conflict which saw 55,573 of his fellow aircrew give their lives in the cause of freedom can only be wondered at. Leslie is a lot more interested in other people's stories than he is in telling his own so after a number of years I was really pleased when I got the opportunity to play a small part in turning his experiences into something which is truly deserving of a real hero. I am sure anyone reading his story will be inspired and enthralled.

From a friend about a hero.

Gary Mitchell

May 2011

High Flight

Oh! I have slipped the surly bonds of Earth
And danced the skies on laughter-silvered wings;
Sunward I've climbed, and joined the tumbling mirth
Of sun-split clouds—and done a hundred things
You have not dreamed of—wheeled and soared and
swung
High in the sunlit silence. Hov'ring there,
I've chased the shouting wind along, and flung
My eager craft through footless halls of air....

Up, up the long, delirious burning blue
I've topped the wind-swept heights with easy grace
Where never lark, or ever eagle flew—
And, while with silent, lifting mind I've trod
The high, untresspassed sanctity of space,
Put out my hand, and touched the face of God.

**Pilot Officer John Gillespie Magee Jr. RAF.
Died 11th December 1941.**

*Dedicated to all those young men of both sides who took
off and never returned home.*

Chapter One
Prologue. 1936.

The young boy stopped ragging his younger brother and together they stared upwards, seeking the source of the noise over their heads. 'There, Leslie, look!' Pointing, the younger of the two indicated eagerly and Leslie Smith followed his brother's finger. Banking smoothly, the Dragon Rapide lost height as it lined up with the runway at Dyce Aerodrome and the two boys watched until it dropped out of sight. Once they were a novelty but now the sight of the frail-looking twin-engined biplane with the glazed nose and glass passenger cabin was a familiar presence over the city of Aberdeen in these pre-war days.

'It must be grand to fly, Jim,' Leslie announced, his glance never wavering from the speck in the sky. 'One day I'm going to be up there, you see.'

'Yeah? Bet you dinna!' answered his brother and together they ran back down Holburn Street towards their home near the Brig O' Dee bar with arms outstretched, noisily imitating airplanes as they hurried back home for their supper.

1944

In the gathering gloom, in a ritual repeated throughout the length of the east coast of England, the sound of revving aero engines pierced the blackness. Large, lumbering four-engined 'Heavies' waddled slowly along the perimeter track to the edge of the flare path, past the small group of WAAFs and ground-crew gathered to watch and wave the aircraft off.

Laden down with their precious cargoes of bombs, fuel and crew, on reaching the runway a quick burst of throttle swung each aircraft onto the centreline of the tarmac where it paused for a moment. After a short pause to scan his instruments the pilot opened the throttles and tested the engines, holding the quivering machine hard against the brakes. Next to him, his Flight Engineer kept a firm hand on all four throttle levers as they waited impatiently to be off. A flashing Aldis lamp from the Control Van gave them clearance and in response brakes were released and the aircraft began its take-off run, gathering speed down the runway. The regal figure of the Station CO cut a commanding figure as he saluted each aircraft accelerating past him down the runway.

Whilst those onboard held their breath, stomachs churning, the dark shape disappeared into the gloom and only the receding sound of aircraft engines and faint glow of navigation lights diminishing to a pinprick told the watchers of a successful take-off as it clawed for attitude and headed towards Occupied Europe. Climbing steadily on their planned heading they reached the allotted altitude, to be joined by others above and below as they merged into that phenomenon known as the Bomber Stream and headed out across a blacked-out Britain towards their intended target.

Soon, almost too soon, another ritual would take place, that of hundreds of heavily-laden aircraft being drawn in to the flickering, probing searchlights, nightfighters and flame-tipped 'flak' from the German anti-aircraft guns like moths to a candle's flame.

In June 1942 the chances of completing a tour of thirty operations with Bomber Command were 25%, just one in four. By December 1944 those odds had risen to 75%, a great improvement as the enemy was driven back and his defences overwhelmed but by the war's end the RAF had lost 70,253 personnel, 55,573 deaths being Bomber Command aircrew. A further 8,000 Bomber Command deaths occurred in training accidents in contrast with those of the Great War where 7,000 of the approximately 14,000 deaths of pilots occurred in training. The World

War Two figures equate to a 44.4% loss rate out of the 125,000 aircrew estimated to have participated in bombing operations over Europe.

Also added to those figures must be 9,800 bomber aircrew who would find themselves languishing as prisoners-of war, lucky survivors of often harrowing combats over the target. Their average age was twenty-two yet many aircraft captains were young men only nineteen years old, baby-faced youths who were amused to be quizzed about their age in many a village pub.

Last but definitely not least, also taken into account must be the 12,570 ground crew and WAAF's who also lost their lives, mainly from enemy raids on the British airfields during the war's early years.

At the start of the war, Britain's effective bomber force numbered only 23 squadrons of twin-engined aircraft. Blenheims, Hampdens, Whitleys and Wellingtons bore the initial burden with raids on the German naval units and leaflet drops (Known as NICKEL raids.) over the continent being the norm. By early 1941 most were being phased out as the new four-engined aircraft came off the assembly lines. The Handley Page Halifax, Short Stirling and the most famous of them all, the Avro Lancaster which entered service in 1942, would become household names in the years to come.

There was no magic formula to survival in the air, no special routine that would guarantee the completion of one's tour and a welcome respite from the strain of operations. Most aircrew carried their own personal good luck charms or mascots and engaged in strange rituals such as peeing on the tail-wheel before take-off. The stark truth is that many crews 'bought it' on their very first time over Europe, disappearing into the smoke and flames of a city ablaze, never to be seen again. Others found death on their fifth, sixth or, for some unlucky souls, got the 'chop' on their twenty-ninth sortie, just hours away from the safety of a completed tour and a reason to contemplate living again.

Although a tour was nominally thirty operations, the average bomber aircrew life expectancy was twenty-one operations. After that magical figure one could be said to be living on borrowed time. No-one knew when it might be their turn to struggle for survival in a doomed aircraft; luck was the governing factor in keeping one alive, nothing else. The Hand of Fate was arbitrary in its choice of who would meet a fiery end or survive, drenched in sweat, to live through the same experience on another night. To be followed all too soon by yet another.

Is there a single factor that defines courage? Can it be classed as the white-hot rage that enables a man to rise up under intense fire and charge into Hell without a moment's hesitation, or the ice-cold determination needed in defusing an unexploded bomb whilst all the time acutely aware that the clock is, literally, ticking down?

During the six years of World War Two, nightly the young men of Britain and its Commonwealth crawled into their allotted positions in a thin, metal cocoon and prepared to face both the enemy and their own fears. In the dead of night, fleets of aircraft and their crews navigated their way over a silent countryside below on flights lasting between six and eight hours, sometimes even longer, not knowing if they would survive the night's action and see the welcoming dawn of an English morning. Each member of every one of those aircraft's crews knew the sobering statistics governing their chances of survival yet all were volunteers, proud to wear the insignia of aircrew on their battledress.

Stifling their own fears they operated as a crew, mindful of each others needs and attributes, the bonding that carried them freezing and oxygen-deprived to the target and back lasting a lifetime for the lucky few who would survive. To live through the fear and anxiety of thirty take-offs and landings, the smell of fuel, dope and the tang of cordite from a flak near-miss took extraordinary courage, fortitude and to a large extent, luck. To survive a tour of thirty operations was a remarkable feat. Leslie Smith completed thirty-eight such operations. This is his story.

Leslie Bruce Smith was born on 29th November 1922, the second son of four boys to William and Mary Smith. The family lived at 637 Holburn Street in Aberdeen where Leslie's father worked as a Fitter's Mate at the Electrical Works in Millburn Street, now part of the Hydro Board. William senior had served in Mesopotamia during the Great War and suffered wounds which possibly contributed to his early death in 1942 at the age of 42.

The family was much respected and well known in the area as Leslie's father was a direct relative of the Smith known as 'The Silver King', an entrepreneur and adventurer who had made a fortune in the silver mines of South America. A modest legacy shared out amongst all the relatives enabled the Smiths of Holburn Street to live life a little easier amidst the financial troubles of the Thirties. Like all boys, Mary Smith's sons got into their fair share of scrapes but their home life was a happy one, centred around loving parents.

All four boys would eventually enter the services. The eldest, William, entered the army, serving in the Royal Artillery whilst Leslie and his other two brothers would serve in the RAF. Leslie served with 61 and 97 Squadrons whilst James went on to become an air gunner on Liberators. Charles, the youngest, entered the RAF just before the war's end but was not called to Active Service.

Leslie attended Skene Street Primary School along with his brothers. He passed the entrance exam for the Robert Gordon School but failed to win a Bursary. As the fees in those days were £10 a month, a steep amount for any family to find, Leslie contented himself with attending Ruthrieston Secondary School. During that time he would rise early with his basket to deliver morning rolls in the Abergeldie/Balmoral area of Aberdeen for bakers, Mitchell and Muil.

A member of the 7th Boys Brigade, Leslie attended Gilcomstoun Kirk on many an occasion. Eager to leave school as soon as he was able, in 1937 at the age of fifteen he became a Butcher's Assistant with the Northern Co-Operative Society in Berryden Road, leading to three years in the butchery trade and attending evening classes to learn more. At one point during his formative years Leslie harboured hopes of becoming an Auctioneer but the war put paid to any chance of progressing in that direction.

Harbouring a keen interest in anything to do with aviation, on 23rd June 1939 at the age of sixteen, Leslie joined the Air Defence Cadet Corps, being inducted by Sqn leader McIntosh into No 151 Aberdeen Squadron in Fairfield House, Fonthill Road. The Air Defence Cadet Corps was established in 1938 to foster the spirit of aviation in young men and in 1939 an ADCC was set up in April of that year in Aberdeen. Named 107 (Aberdeen) Squadron it was affiliated to 612 (County of Aberdeen) Squadron RAF. In May the same year applications were received from over 200 boys between the ages of 14-18 and after interviews and medicals were carried out, 107 Squadron came into being. As demand for places outstripped the number of places available, 151 Sqn ATC and 1741 Sqn ATC were also formed in Aberdeen to give more young men the chance to savour a taste of aviation. By the outbreak of war 172 ADCC's had been established across Britain, giving the RAF a valuable source of recruits.

Leslie joined the latter, 151 Sqn ATC and later became one of 400,000 cadets who would go on to join the RAF when war broke out. Possessed of a musical bent he played the kettle drum in the Fife and Drum section, attended lectures, drills and also received a grounding in aircraft recognition, something that would aid him in his flying career in later years. The many admiring glances from young Aberdeen 'quines' at him dressed in his Air defence Corps clothing confirmed a long-held belief that all women looked favourably on a man in uniform but a degree of self-consciousness at that time held him back from any notable conquests. A lot of time was taken up by his love of roller-skating, a sport he was to become a past master in.

The rise of the Nazi Party in Germany in the 1930's, under their charismatic leader, Adolf Hitler, meant that Leslie would not be a butcher for very long. On taking power in 1933, Hitler's first action was to build up the strength of her armed forces, investing in modern aircraft designs and military hardware. Alarmed at Germany's rearming and open aggression, Britain began a hectic programme of strengthening and expanding its armed forces, the result being that when war was declared in September 1939 following Germany's invasion of Poland, the Royal Air Force could field modern fighters such as the Spitfire and Hurricane.

More attention was paid to fighter acquisition, partly due to politician Stanley Baldwin's famous dictum in 1932 that 'the bomber would always get through'. As a result of this blinkered thinking bomber development was watered down in the race to produce more fighters. The bomber types that were produced tended to be light, twin-engined aircraft that lacked the bomb-carrying capacity and, apart from the Vickers Wellington, the range to inflict much damage on Germany at the outbreak of hostilities.

The storm clouds gathering over Europe had alerted the population to the trials and tribulations ahead and when war broke out, with his love of flying and determination to

13

become a pilot, Leslie volunteered immediately for the RAF but was placed on the reserve list, joining the Air Defence League whilst he curbed his impatience. Their elder brother, William had enlisted in the Royal Artillery and was to die as a Prisoner-of-War in Changi POW camp in Singapore.

Gunner 919621 William Urquhart Smith was just twenty-one when he was captured by the Japanese on the 15th February 1942 at the surrender of Singapore. His unit, the 80th Anti-tank Regiment of the Royal Artillery, had initially landed in Singapore in November 1941 and fought its way down the Malayan Peninsula. Part of the 53rd Brigade, during the retreat to the island fortress they used their 48 two-pounder anti-tank guns to great effect before surrendering with the rest of the garrison on the island of Singapore.

On surrendering with his unit, he was interned in the Changi prisoner-of-war camp where he was known to have died on 11th September 1942. He has no known grave and is remembered like so many others on the Kranji War Memorial in Singapore.

The opening year of the war passed into the New Year of 1940, with no end in sight to hostilities. Rationing was introduced in January and the 'Phoney War' was underway on the continent with Allied forces dug in along the frontiers. Germany used the time to build up her strength after the actions in Poland and Czechoslovakia, content to play a waiting game until she was ready to unleash her forces against the British, French and Belgian armies opposing her.

During that time the RAF carried out several more NICKEL raids on Germany but public protest at their dropping only leaflets on the German population whilst German aircraft bombed Warsaw saw a drastic reduction in this type of raid. RAF aircraft continued to seek out the German naval fleet in daylight but a disastrous raid on Wilhelmshaven on 18th December, 1939, when 12 out of 22 Wellingtons were easily shot down by Messerschmitt Bf 109 fighters brought home the need to redefine the RAF's role.

In April 1940, Germany overran Denmark and used that country as a stepping stone to invade Norway. The RAF sent several squadrons of aircraft, such as the then obsolete Gloster Gladiator fighter but Norway proved impossible to defend and she would surrender in May. On the 12th April the RAF carried out the biggest daylight raid of the war so far when a force of 83 Blenheims, Hampdens and Wellingtons attacked naval targets in Kristiansand harbour. The raid highlighted the fact that the British bombers were too slow and too lightly armed to fight off modern fighters with six Hampdens and three Wellingtons being shot down easily by the defending fighters.

Another tragedy in the campaign occurred when many RAF aircrew and groundcrew were amongst 1,200 men killed when the aircraft carrier, HMS Glorious, was sank in the North Sea returning from Norway on 8th June by the German battleships *Scharnhorst* and *Gneisenau*.

On May 10th 1940, the German Wehrmacht smashed its way into both Holland and then Belgium. Holland sued for peace on the 14th, Belgium held out until the 27th. France was attacked at the same time and after initial successes the Allied armies fell back before the German *Blitzkrieg* tactics and the British Expeditionary Force retreated to the coast in June where over 334,000 troops were eventually evacuated in the 'Miracle of Dunkirk.'

The RAF suffered greatly during the Battle of France but the decision made by Sir Hugh Dowding of Fighter Command in not releasing more squadrons of fighters such as the Hurricane and Spitfire to serve in that conflict was to pay dividends when the Battle of Britain started later that year.

The British strategic bombing campaign against Germany can be said to have commenced on the night of 15/16th May 1940 when a force of 96 aircraft, mainly Hampdens, Whitleys and Wellingtons attacked targets in the Ruhr. The indiscriminate bombing of Rotterdam by the Germans the day before was the deciding factor by the RAF in abandoning attacks on what were considered military targets to the west of the Rhine and beginning an all-out assault on industrial targets to the east. The crews were left to their own devices to work out their own route to the target and return home, in stark contrast to the multi-thousand aircraft fleets in later years flying to and from their targets in strictly-defined conditions of altitude and heading.

On 10th June 1940, Italy entered the conflict under the leadership of 'IL Duce', Benito Mussolini by declaring war on Britain and France. Italian aircraft would take part in the Battle of Britain but for the most part the Italians concentrated their military efforts in the Western Desert.

Aberdeen was to be no stranger to the war herself, bearing the brunt of several raids by German aircraft of *Luftflotte 5* operating from its bases in Norway. On 12th July 1940, a Heinkel He111 H-3 of *9/KG26*, piloted by Leutnant Herbert Huck and operating from Stavanger-Sola set off on a mission to bomb Leuchars airfield in Fife, with the town of Broughty Ferry near Dundee as its secondary target. It was intercepted near the North-East coast and attacked by 603 Sqn Spitfires piloted by P/O J.Caister, P/O K.Gilroy and Sgt. K. Arber, falling in flames onto the ice-rink then under construction on South Anderson Drive in Aberdeen. Many of Aberdeen's citizens having their lunch that day stared open-mouthed as the stricken aircraft carrying the registration code *1H+FT* dipped low over the city wreathed in flames before crashing and exploding in a fireball less than half a mile away from where Leslie and his family were living in Holburn Street. All four crew members of the Heinkel were killed and are buried in Dyce Churchyard.

In attempting to escape its pursuers the aircraft had opened its bomb bay as it fled across Aberdeen, the bombs landing on Hall Russell's shipyard by Footdee killing several dozen workers. Other bombs damaged Hogg and Co in Regent Quay and the Nelson Bar. Further raids on Aberdeen followed, culminating on the severe raid of April 1943 and the family Anderson Shelter behind the stairs of 637 Holburn St was soon well-used.

Just as dusk was gathering in the evening of 21st April 1943, the citizens of Aberdeen were alarmed to see the sight of 30 German bombers, Dornier Do217's of *Kampfgeschwader 2* sweep in across the city from the North Sea. The bombers, members of a unit stationed in Holland, had flown to Stavanger in Norway where they were refuelled and bombed-up for the flight across the North Sea to Aberdeen.

Commanded by *Oberst* Dietrich Peltz, the German airman of *KG2* were on a revenge mission, a payback for the damage inflicted by the RAF on German cities. It was decided to make a show of force against the British Isles and Aberdeen was selected as a target. Roaring across the city the Do217's dropped their bombs indiscriminately, spraying the streets with machine-gun fire as they did so. Woodside, Kittybrewster and Hilton were particularly hard hit and a single 500kg bomb landing on Bedford Road killed 19 people. The Postmaster of Woodside perished with his family when another bomb struck their home, demolishing it entirely.

A young German airman, Gerhard Rohrbach, described his part in the raid as follows: '...I was a corporal, one of the crew of four in a twin-engined Dornier 217, a variation of the Do17...We were lucky...lucky as we never were before and never afterwards. There was no defence—or, when there was, it was not worth mentioning. We arrived at dusk, barely thirty metres above the waves, and at first our gunners attacked the anti-aircraft emplacements, whose shocked crews were trying to get into position. I well remember the old harbour, and this broad Union Street leading into Aberdeen city, and an amused crowd of unsuspecting people leaving a cinema.

Soon all was fire and crashes and explosions. After we dropped our bombs, our pilot climbed in a hurry and turned and set his course back to Stavanger. We had only limited fuel and no additional tanks, and we were afraid we wouldn't reach our base within the calculated time.

I don't know where our bombs fell. But on the next day, when it was warm enough to allow us crewmen to swim in the sea, we heard clearly on BBC radio that we had provoked one of the worst disasters.

We were happy. A job was done. And when we called it a good job, we meant that for the first time none of our people was killed or wounded and we had lost no planes. At Stavanger, our aircraft were refuelled and, without having any sleep, our KG2—some 40 bombers in all—went back to the Netherlands airbase.....'

In all, 98 civilians perished, along with 27 servicemen who died when bombs struck the Gordon Barracks and over 200 civilians were wounded. A large number of bombs failed to explode, a direct cause of being dropped too low for the fuses to operate properly. The attackers fled out to sea leaving a trail of death and destruction behind them, flying back to Norway without loss.

Not for nothing was Aberdeen nicknamed 'Siren City', one of the most frequently bombed cities in Scotland. She endured 32 attacks from the *Luftwaffe* with over 13,000 houses suffering damage ranging from slight to many which were completely destroyed. High explosives as well as incendiaries were dropped by the German bombers causing more than 200 deaths and many injuries.

During the summer and early autumn of 1940 the Battle of Britain raged as the beleaguered British Isles reeled under the onslaught of the German *Luftwaffe*. British resistance stiffened and the populace were heartened to read of the RAF's exploits in destroying many of the enemy aircraft and their escort fighters which sought to bomb British airfields and military installations into submission. 15th September 1940 proved to be a turning point when 185 German aircraft were claimed destroyed by the RAF and anti-aircraft guns, breaking the resolve and morale of the *Luftwaffe* crews facing them.

Another turning point was a navigational mistake which led to the bombing of London by German bombers on the 24th August 1940. In retaliation, the following day 50 RAF bombers, mainly Wellingtons, bombed Berlin. A furious Hitler ordered the flattening of London in revenge and the *Luftwaffe's* efforts switched from military to attacks on civilian targets. The error on the German's part gave RAF Fighter Command a much-needed breathing space from the constant losses in men and aircraft they'd suffered and this respite was a major factor in the defeat of the Germans in the air war over Britain in 1940.

On the 7th September, 300 German bombers escorted by 600 fighters devastated a huge swathe of London. The London Blitz of the winter of 1940 and into 1941 had begun, culminating in the firestorm raid of 29th December when the *Luftwaffe* dropped over 1,000 bombs on London. Other cities, towns and villages throughout Britain,

Aberdeen included, were to suffer under nightly raids and indiscriminate bombing. Glasgow, Liverpool, Southampton and Swansea, amongst many others, would all feel the wrath of the German bombs on their cities.

Throughout these months, curbing his impatience, Leslie continued to work as a butcher, all the while fretting to join the action. Life had changed dramatically during the opening months of the war, with the Blackout, rationing and lack of socialising all playing their part in the loss of what had passed for a normal life. In spite of the lack of what had previously passed for the luxuries of life there was a great camaraderie to be found, with many a night of Bothy Ballads and sing-songs aimed to keep one's spirits up.
When asked why he volunteered, Leslie answered:

'Like many young men of the time, I saw the rise of the Nazi's in Germany as something evil and joining the services made me feel as if I was doing my bit in helping the oppressed.
My father predicted that Hitler was leading the German nation to war and would involve Europe in a war of gigantic proportions. A soldier who had been severely injured by shrapnel in the World War One debacle in Mesopotamia, he was hopeful that his progeny would avoid such privations.'

His mother's anxiety at having one son already overseas as a serving soldier was tempered by his father's pride when at last, in late March 1941, a buff-coloured envelope dropped through the family letter-box. The envelope heralded the call for Leslie to travel to Edinburgh to the RAF Assessment Centre on 2nd April as a prelude to his call-up.

20

With a packed lunch in his pocket he boarded the train in Aberdeen Station and proceeded the 150 miles down the East Coast to Edinburgh. The tests would necessitate an overnight stay and at the Assessment Centre he was tested in Morse and basic radio-telephonic knowledge, his time in the Air Cadet Corps standing him in good stead. From there he progressed through to a severe medical examination, a not-too severe IQ test, more intelligence tests and finally a colour blindness test. No results were given and he left the following day, travelling the return journey back to Aberdeen in a state of frustration and anxiety as to whether or not he would pass selection.

A confidence-jolting letter soon followed, informing him that he had been turned down for pilot training due to 'poor ocular balance.' The bad news was tempered by the offer of aircrew acceptance in another category and Leslie opted for that of WOP/AG, wireless operator/air gunner. It was to be another six months of waiting until he heard again from the War office but finally, on the 2nd October, he arrived at RAF Padgate near Warrington, Lancashire, to join other young men of his intake and begin his RAF training at No.3 Recruitment Centre there.

During his waiting, much had happened on the war front. The nation was shocked when on 24th May 1941, HMS Hood, the biggest battle-cruiser in the world, was sunk in the Denmark Strait off Iceland by the German battleship DKS Bismarck with the loss of over 1,400 men. The German seamen did not have long to savour her triumph. Bismarck's quest to attack allied convoys in the Atlantic lasted only a few more days before she was hunted down and sunk by a combined force of Swordfish torpedo aircraft and heavy units of the Royal Navy, taking with her to the bottom over 2,000 of her crew. Only 115 shocked survivors were plucked from the icy waters before a U-boat alert halted any more rescue attempts by the British ships.

The U-Boat menace had also begun to make its presence felt as the Germans sought to bring mainland Britain to its knees by cutting off its lifeline, the supplies brought in by the Atlantic convoys. In 1939, U-boats sank a total of 114 merchant ships with a tonnage of 421,000 tons but by the end of 1940 shipping totalling over 2 million tons had been sunk.

On the 22nd June 1941 Hitler made what was to be his biggest mistake in the war, the invasion of Russia by the armies of the *Wehrmacht*. Initial successes and huge amounts of territories gained would entice millions of German soldiers further and further into the Russian hinterland where a fierce arctic winter would decimate them on the road to Moscow. The fighting there would be the most savage known as both sides engaged in a brutal campaign that would last for another four years.

The war that was confined mainly to Europe and the Western deserts of Africa took on a wider aspect when on the 7th December 1941, in a deadly surprise attack, 183 Japanese aircraft devastated the American naval port of Pearl harbour, a lagoon in the Hawaiian islands.

Launched from six aircraft carriers, the bombs and torpedoes of the Japanese sank four battleships, damaged another four and sank or damaged several cruisers and destroyers, American losses amounting to over 2,400 men. Unfortunately for the Japanese, none of the American carriers were in harbour at the time, a crucial fact that would gain in importance in the months and years to come.

America let no time pass before responding to what American President, Franklin D Roosevelt called: *'A date which will live in infamy.'* As Japan had already declared war to coincide with the attack, America and her allies, including Britain, declared war on Japan the following day.

America further declared war on Germany and her allies, making the conflict a World War.

As these events unfolded, Aircraftsman 2nd Class Smith found waiting for him a maelstrom of queues for this and that, uniforms, haircuts, drill and documentation, all the while being harassed by unfriendly NCO's who badgered and bullied their charges into obeying without question. Leslie's natural sense of logic was overwhelmed by these men's desire to submerge the raw recruits under a mountain of threats for lateness, slovenliness impertinence (real or imagined.) and he felt a great sense of loneliness.

However, the hostility he encountered at the recruitment centre was brief and after being imbued with a sense of belonging he was on his way with several other new recruits to No.3 Signal School based in Blackpool.

For a young man who'd not spent many nights away from the closeness of this family before these early days were among the hardest he would encounter but he knuckled down and gradually came to terms with the strangeness of the situation. He learnt to remember his service number (1346377) and bawl it out on demand. The Winter Gardens and Burton Building were used to hold briefing assemblies and he soon realised the need to comply with all he was taught, a wise decision as it turned out.

At Blackpool, in the Signal School located on the top floor of the Woolworths building, a foundation of basic telegraphy was laid for speeds of an acceptable level, built up by letters of the alphabet in letter groups and punctuation. Simple electrical circuitry was explained, key manipulation, transmitting and receiving exercises completed and examinations passed.

The opening Morse requirement was four words per minute, building up to a final requirement of twelve words per minute. A keen sense of rhythm was needed to receive and understand Morse and many were eliminated at this stage, only 20% of the intake surviving, among them a proud and relieved Leslie Smith. Examinations were conducted in the Burton building, in a converted ballroom and great numbers of aspiring W/Op's would suffer the nerves of 'Morse Madness' as they waited for their turn to be tested. The men that failed were sent for General Duties and many a rumour was concocted to keep those remaining recruits noses to the grindstone. From these experiences was born a term all recruits who passed through Blackpool remembered for the rest of their lives, *'Gone for a Burton.'*

Memories of his days in Blackpool include the friendship of fellow recruits, amongst them Jackie Patterson (A boxer of renown.) and Danny Gliddon (A well-known footballer.) Of Palatine Road, Squires Gate, upstairs and downstairs at Burtons, the swimming baths. Fall in, form fours, salute, dismiss, pressed uniforms, more haircuts, in fact all the panoply of a service attempting to make something solid from the raw material it had been given.

One memory that still stands out down the years was hearing the voice of another friend, Taffy Evans, practice the song "How deep is the night." as he prepared to appear in the Winter Garden with Max Bygraves, Nat Jackly and Max Miller in a Command Performance. Fifteen years later, Leslie and Taffy Evans would meet up again in the Tivoli Gardens in Aberdeen when Leslie was invited for a reunion backstage.

After Blackpool, the delights of No.3 Signal School in Compton Basset, Wiltshire beckoned and Leslie arrived on a fresh morning on the 29th January 1942 to begin the serious business of training to be a Wireless Operator. Here, both Ground and Aircrew Wireless Operators were trained in a professional and quite intense thirteen week course. Again, as at Blackpool, many flunked the course and were sent away, Leslie puts his powers of retention as a deciding factor in his success in passing all set out before him:

'Compton Basset offered many opportunities to socialise and I set about attempting to take part in as many activities as possible, playing cards, badminton and taking up long distance running to develop more physical strength. Although the camp abounded with many WAAF's, an innate shyness prevented me from engaging any in serious conversations and I tended to stay away from the camp bar and dance hall. Stern lectures from my parents on the consequences of contracting a venereal disease from strange women had had its effect on my confidence so I attempted to stay clear of any situation that could lead to a relationship.'

German aircraft periodically ranged over the Wiltshire countryside, dropping bombs on many military establishments and Compton Basset didn't escape their attentions. The sound of the air-raid siren would send them all scurrying for the shelters and many a love-affair had its beginnings in such a setting.

Those airmen considered suitable for aircrew were allowed to wear the arm cloth badge of a W/OP and were also issued with white flashes for their forage caps. This sense of being different gave a fresh impetus to their studies and the long course was finally ended by the taking of their final exams.

When the posting's were announced Leslie was disappointed to find he would be travelling to RAF Castletown in the far north of Scotland, near Thurso, the next stop while he waited for the call to start his aircrew wireless operator training. The stuffy train journey up through England and over the border into Scotland brought him nearer home and a welcome spot of leave before reporting to a bleak Castletown on the 5th May 1942 as an Aircraftsman 1st Class.

Recognising the lack off defences in the far north of Scotland the land at Castletown became the subject of compulsory purchase under the Emergency Powers Act in 1939 and by May 1940 the new fighter aerodrome had been finished, joining 13 Group of Fighter Command:

'As accommodation on the aerodrome was limited we were billeted within buildings in the vicinity. Castlehill House by the harbour became the HQ and Officers Mess whilst several other buildings, two of the local schools, the Drill Hall and the Masonic Hall amongst them were taken over as accommodation for the airmen. Myself and the detachment of signallers I joined were billeted and worked at the Masonic Hall which was situated between Wick and Thurso, commanded by a Flying Officer who resided in Castlehill House. The unit boasted a PBX, a telephone exchange covering 13 Group and a TR1154/55 radio set for communication. The 1154/55 sets were a general-purpose Marconi transmitter/receiver having direction-finding facilities and a built-in generator driven by a 24-volt battery. It was a set I would become very familiar with, being the standard airborne radio T/R fitted to Lancasters.

The unit discipline was not harsh, the sleeping quarters shared by a crew of 18/20 men overseen by disinterested corporals who could be easily bribed. My duties including taking a turn in listening out for calls whilst Q and X code signals were dealt with for navigational and signal strength assessment. Aircraft recognition and radar equipment at local sites was also under our remit, giving a welcome break from the boring humdrum tediousness of it all.

A popular location was that at Meikle Bay where a farm family treated the servicemen regally and I managed to indulge in a mild flirtation with one of the daughters, a pretty girl named Daisy. Sports were encouraged and well-supported and the addition of a camp cinema in 1942 was a welcome venue to relax in.'

During the summer of 1942 many VIP's passed through the aerodrome, including a surprise visit by Prince Bernhardt of the Netherlands in his Spitfire. Unfortunately, he misjudged his approach and landed the aircraft on its nose causing severe damage but escaping unharmed himself.

Life passed all too slowly, although Leslie headed for home from time to time to a fine welcome from his family. One such visit was to be tinged with grief when his father succumbed to a heart attack, brought on by a 70-mile round trip on bicycles from Aberdeen to Longside. Father and son completed the trip but a stiff breeze encountered on the return leg was to prove fatal for William Smith senior.

One repercussion of that sad event was that his mother left Aberdeen to become the Housekeeper for the Commanding Officer of Fort George near Nairn for the remainder of the war, a reminder that grief in wartime is not only reserved for those serving in the forces. Leslie spent many of his leaves with his mother, travelling up from Kings Cross Station in London and staying with his cousins and their parents on Flemington Farm, Ardersier, in order to be closer to her.

The winter of 1942/43 was particularly savage and the train line to Wick from Inverness was blocked for a considerable period. Privation affected the station and with rations running low, an airdrop of ... bully beef...was effected and became their staple diet. Served hot, cold, naked, battered, mashed, the sight and smell haunts Leslie to this day.

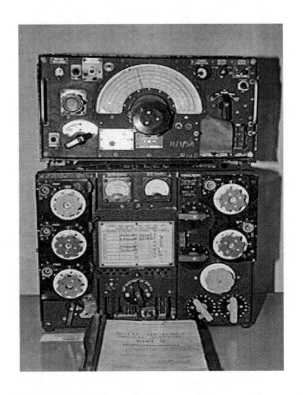

The R1155/T1154 radio transmitter-receiver sets fitted to Lancasters during WW2.
(Photograph and information below courtesy of Wikipedia).

The R1155/T1154 combination radio transmitter-receiver was one found fitted to many aircraft of WW2, the Lancaster in particular. It was a piece of equipment that Leslie would come to know and use to great effect throughout his operational career. The sets operated on the High Frequency band (HF) up to 30Mhz and the transmitter used Amplitude Modulation (AM) for speech

28

and a Modulated Continuous Wave (MCW) for Morse transmissions. Besides being able to tune the transmitter manually, the wireless operator could also choose from several pre-selected frequencies. The knobs on the units were shaped in such a manner to allow them to be used whilst wearing thick gloves, a necessity given the extreme cold at which the aircraft operated.

The receiver was also capable of being used in the Direction-Finding mode (DF), allowing the pilot to fly along a beacon transmission bearing using a frequency selected by the wireless operator. During their time aloft, Leslie would utilise the Morse code and speech capabilities of the sets to relay changes in flight paths, targets, targets and return instructions to the pilot and navigator.

Chapter Two

At last the longed-for day arrived and in March 1943 a newly-promoted 1346377 Leading Aircraftsman Smith was posted to an Initial Training Unit back at his old stamping-ground of Compton Basset.

It would have been a daunting prospect to the poor bewildered 'sprogs' who congregated on a cold March morning to take their first look at the clapped-out aircraft they would undergo training in. Here in the coming weeks they were to be transformed into airborne Wireless Operators, utilising ancient twin-engined bi-planes such as the Fairey Dragon Rapide, renamed the 'Dominie' for RAF purposes:

'Drawing bulky aircrew clothing and parachutes we'd be jammed, six at a time into the cold and draughty fuselage and take to the air in a series of judders and lurching movements that brought fear to us all. Six work-tops had been attached next to flimsy seats and here we trainees would work furiously, earphones on, listening out for the faint messages we were to translate and log. With no windows to give an outside view of the world and provide a reference, airsickness and anxiety was something to get used to, swallowing the bile and the fear inherent in such flights.

First impressions? Cold, the overwhelming smell of doped fuselages, engine oil and the sweet stench of high-octane fuel. All these crowded in on one's existence and left a lingering smell that was hard to eradicate. The heart-stopping fear as the aircraft shuddered and dropped suddenly and most importantly of all, the fear of failure. To be 'washed-out' at this early stage would have been a negation of all that I'd striven for so I clung grimly on, literally, and steadily worked my way through the flights and exercises.

Impatient instructors coupled with indifferent pilots, all took their toll on young men's courage and endurance. The mysteries and power of the trailing aerial was drummed into us and working a ratchet device we sweated to lower the aerial down its tube, weighted with lead to stabilise it outside in the slipstream of the aircraft. The action was governed by a release handle which was difficult to operate and it was at this point you'd feel the anger of the instructor if frozen fingers failed to release it to his satisfaction. And pity the poor trainee who committed the cardinal sin of forgetting to wind it in prior to landing!'

After weeks of suffering the fears and anxieties of this cramped existence, Leslie's solo RT flight was carried out in a Proctor. Flown by pilots resting between tours the aircraft would be tossed around the skies in the most alarming and nonchalant manner as each aspiring W/Op was tested to the limit. It was under these circumstances that Leslie's calm temperament came to the fore and he was able to ignore the distractions and successfully follow all the instructions given to him over the intercom. On landing he had the satisfaction of knowing that he had been tested and passed another hurdle on his way towards the real thing.

All too soon this phase came to an end and at the end of May a railway ticket was handed to him, this time involving a long journey through England and Scotland to the far North and an eight-week gunnery course at No.8 Airborne Gunnery School based at RAF Evanton, Tain, in Rosshire.

RAF Evanton was situated in Alness Bay, a mile or so outside Tain on the Cromarty Firth. The remoteness of its location was made up by the magnificence of its scenery, high snow-laden mountains to the west contrasting vividly with the flatland near the coast. The local beaches had their outlines spoiled by thousands of sharp stakes embedded in them to stop a German airborne invasion should they attempt such a landing but this obvious blight on the landscape detracted little from the overall scenery when viewed from aloft.

Tain was a small and pleasant highland town with enough bars such as the Balnagowan Arms and the Royal Hotel to meet the needs of thirsty aircrew as they wandered around its streets. Inverness was a two-hour train ride away for those lucky enough to be given a leave pass but for the most part, life revolved around the airbase and the demands that learning their trade as airborne gunners brought:

'After kitting up, we'd position ourselves in the primitive turrets of Blackburn Botha bombers which bore the nickname of "Flying Coffins" owing to several fatal crashes and take-off over the Firth to engage cloth drogues towed behind Westland Lysander aircraft. Here the workings of the twin Browning .303 machine-gun turret became less of a mystery as we fired burst after burst at the targets and learnt how to deal with stoppages and guns jamming. Cine cameras fitted to the guns showed us visually how accurate we were and our aim improved as a result of this innovation.

Deflection firing, the different tracer patterns, gun synchronisation ('harmonisation', as it was sometimes known.), drogues, all of these became familiar as the aircraft dived and weaved, practising the standard method of escape that would become second nature in the air, that of the dreaded 'corkscrew.' Turret hydraulics were explained and thoroughly drummed into us as we worked methodically through the intensive course.

The .303 Browning machine-guns in aircraft use at the time were stripped and reassembled by us until we could perform the task blind-folded if necessary, a preamble to possibly having to do it in the air in darkness and under fire. We did all our work with bare hands to begin with and then had to learn how to clear stoppages, load ammunition belts etc whilst wearing gloves. To try and do this type of work at altitude would have meant skin being stripped from bare hands due to the intense cold.

It was at Tain that my comrades and I were introduced to more modern aircraft such as the single-engined Boulton Paul Defiant equipped with a rear turret that had caused such consternation to the Luftwaffe when they first encountered them. From below they looked like Hurricanes and the Luftwaffe suffered heavy losses against the Defiant before they realised the aircraft's forward-firing armament was non-existent. The Defiant was swiftly switched to the nightfighter role before being relegated as a training aircraft. A twin-engined light bomber, the Douglas A-20 Boston was also sometimes encountered, an aircraft I never quite warmed to.'

With this phase successfully passed, the awarding of the Wireless Operator/Air Gunner's brevet followed. Leslie was now deemed ready for his final training. Another railway ticket and a lengthy journey on a draughty, crowded train saw him arrive on the 3rd August 1943 at the gates of No 9(O) Advanced Flying Unit (AFU.) based at Llandwrog in North Wales.

Four miles SE of Caernarvon, Llandwrog was situated in a pleasant location beside the Irish Sea, nestling as it did in the shadows of Snowdonia. An Air Gunnery School was based there before the Observers Flying School opened there in 1943. Being below sea level with the waters held back by a dyke, the concrete runways made for safe and easy flying although take-offs and landings were always interesting. The aircraft used here for advanced training were twin-engined Avro Ansons, a communications, sometime bomber, aircraft.

Leslie soon found himself in a hotch-potch of nationalities. Australia, New Zealand, Canada, Jamaica, South Africa and India, all the countries of the Commonwealth were represented, as well as others from Occupied Europe, Poland and Czechoslovakia. All with one goal, to pass through their training here and go on to flying operations.

With such a mix of nationalities and personalities many firm, lasting friendships were formed as the common bond of training drew them together. Some friendships were brief as poor flying skills, poor maintenance and bad weather took its toll of those gathered there in the following weeks, a grim reminder that they were all engaged in a deadly game.

'It wasn't all doom and gloom, life had its lighter side too. There were sports to take up and Caernarvon with its pubs and hotels, in particular the Prince of Wales, was only a short ride away. Some men ruthlessly pursued the many local, pretty females but for most of us celibacy was the rule. The fear of entering into a relationship and the heartache that could follow made us keep that sort of life at arms length, many of us preferring the stark comfort of the Sergeants Mess to the delights beckoning only a few miles away.'

Tiring flights over the Irish Sea, overflying Northern Ireland and as far up as the Isle of Man were spent in assimilating all the instruction given and putting it to good use as the aircraft laboriously flew them round and round whilst they practised their airborne radio skills. More examinations were taken and passed, another milestone reached. It was at Llandwrog that the aircrew were informed as to which type of unit they would be progressing to. Some went to Coastal Command; some to Transport Command but the cream of the W/Op's were destined for Bomber Command, Leslie Smith amongst them.

Before completing his training at Llandwrog, Leslie suffered a setback in September when, he suffered a fall, necessitating a seven-week stay in No.2 Airmens Convalescent Depot at RAF Hospital Hoylake, Merseyside. He recalled wryly that:

'I'd been returning from a weekend leave blissfully cuddled up to a nubile WAAF on the overnight train down from Aberdeen and on stopping at Crewe had gallantly dashed impetuously down the platform to procure a hot cup of tea for my female companion. Unfortunately, a large gentleman blocked my path and in my haste I failed to spot that he was pulling a trailer loaded down with heavy cases. I performed aerial manoeuvres that would not have shamed a circus acrobat as I sailed over the trailer, landing heavily and injuring myself severely in the process. I still bear the resultant scars to this day! My cuddly WAAF travelled blithely on without her human headrest, thirst unquenched and totally unaware of my predicament.'

This might have been a blessing in disguise, given the crew he was to join later and after being discharged he travelled back to Llandwrog in late October 1943 and rejoined the hustle and bustle of flying training. Christmas soon came and went, his only memories of it the battered Christmas Day menu in amongst his remaining treasured wartime possessions. With the completion of his intensive training, Sergeant Leslie Smith was posted in early 1944 to an operational unit at Upper Heyford, the final step towards becoming accepted as a valued member of a bomber's crew.

Dressed in his best blues, proudly wearing his new-won sergeant's stripes and sporting his gas-mask bag nonchalantly over his shoulder, 1346377 Sergeant WOP/AG Leslie Smith passed through the gates of No 16 Operational Training Unit. A torn photograph shows him in the last training class he would be involved with before joining a crew. Here he would finish the final part of his training before being introduced to the men in whose hands, literally, his life would depend and as a crew they would forge a bond that would take them through the fears and anxieties of darkened enemy skies to the peace beyond that awaited them.

Over the next months, Leslie and the other WOP/AG's making up his course flew in a variety of aircraft as they concentrated hard on the complexities of communication duties within an airborne combat environment. It was here that he came face to face with the mighty Lancaster's predecessor the Manchester, his flying hours total increasing with flights in this unlucky aircraft and other RAF stalwarts such as the Stirling and Wellington. All this was in preparation for the day when they would be passed fit to become part of an operational crew.

The prize for passing was ones own 'Observer's and Air Gunners Logbook' together with the direst of warnings should it be lost or defaced as it constituted a secret document. Every month, they would fill in the relevant pages and have the Flight Commander and Squadron Leader endorse it before stowing it in a safe place.

Having passed that final hurdle and in possession of his logbook, Leslie was directed to one of the hangars where he found pilots, navigators, gunners, wireless operators and flight engineers milling around in seeming random confusion. This was one of Bomber Command's masterstrokes. Bomber crews picked themselves, from the great melee of humanity aimlessly wandering around crews would be formed from a quick glance, a pertinent question or just a plain hunch. Pilots dashed around trying to secure for themselves what they perceived to be the pick of the bunch, all in a sense of healthy competition and banter:

'No-one rushed to procure my services but eventually twenty-four crews stood together and with them one Leslie Bruce Smith, safe under the watchful eye of Pilot Officer Harry Brooker. A quiet, taciturn man, Harry Brooker was the epitome of a bomber pilot, easy-going on the ground but once airborne the complete commander. Our crew's survival over the next nine months of flying training and operations were due in no small part to his flying skills.

Harry came from the Harrogate area of Yorkshire and I can still recall the day Harry met his future wife. We were at a show in London when Harry saw a pretty girl in the chorus line. He waited for her after the show finished and introduced himself. Harry and Marge were married when the war ended and returned to a life together in Harrogate.

Completing our crew was navigator Ken Brown, bomb aimer Dave Hector, with 'Jock' D'Arcy air gunner. 'Jock' was a typical Glaswegian, dark with a pencil-thin moustache he kept us all amused with his humorous outlook on life. A great laugh on the ground, in the air he was transformed into a keen and professional member of the crew

Awkward to begin with in each other's company we soon melded into an efficient team under Harry

Brooker's leadership. We flew in Wellingtons to begin with and after being assessed as competent we progressed on to the Stirling, where we were joined by the last two members of our crew. Bill Morgan was to be our Flight Engineer and Paddy our Mid-upper Gunner. Bill was a biscuit company representative in civvy life, a bit older than the rest of the crew but a valued member. Totally professional in the air, once on terra firma he liked his beer and to chase the ladies!

Ken Brown was a Scot from Kelso, in the Borders. A cinema projector operator in civilian life, he was a quiet man who kept pretty much to himself. Precise, well-organised and dedicated to his task, he navigated our aircraft to and from the targets with great efficiency and I remember with gratitude the debt we still all owe him. On two occasions Ken was 'borrowed' by the PFF Mosquitoes for deep-penetration raids as they were well aware of his capabilities but he always came back and went on to complete 34 ops with Harry Brooker and the crew.

Dave Hector was a Cockney who had the novelty of his twin brother also flying as aircrew with 61 Squadron, albeit with a different crew. A fun-loving person with a ready wit, Dave was kindly and conscientious, a good man to have around and a team player in the many sports leagues we found in the local pubs.'

Designed by Short Brothers and featuring a seven-man crew, armed with eight Browning .303 machine-guns the Stirling entered service in 1941. With four Bristol Hercules engines and a maximum payload of 14,000lbs but a low service ceiling of around 16,000ft the Stirling could carry nearly twice the bombs of contemporary twin-engined bombers such as the Vickers Wellington. Larger than the

Halifax and Lancasters which would eventually replace it, it had a shortened wing-span owing to the need to conserve weight. Myths abound that the clipped wings (100ft long.) were this length so the aircraft would fit into a standard RAF hangar but the reality was the need to keep the aircraft's weight down.

The wing was redesigned but a major drawback to the Stirling was its inability to operate at higher altitudes, a feature the German nightfighters easily exploited. The Germans didn't have it all their own way, though. Delighted Stirling pilots found that the redesigned wing gave them a roll rate which allowed them to out-turn German fighters such as the Ju88 and Bf110 but over a third of those produced would be lost in action, totalling 582 with a further 119 Stirlings written-off in training accidents or on landing.

By 1943, many Stirling units had been relegated to training duties although some did carry on in the Pathfinder role. Standing 28 feet tall on its spindly undercarriage, this was the aircraft Harry Brooker and his fledgling crew gazed up at in awe on their first encounter.

'Our lives coalesced into a helter-skelter of circuits and bumps, take-offs and landings, interspersed with numerous cross-country flights as we wrestled with the task of becoming used to acting in harmony as a fully-fledged crew. Briefings, check drills, all contributed to building up our confidence and the hours spent in the circuit flying the Stirling laid the groundwork for the hazardous operational flights looming ever closer.

It was a stable aircraft with a fine view from the cockpit for Harry Brooker. Take-offs were a bit tricky and one had to be careful on landing not to collapse an undercarriage leg but the Stirling gave us the confidence to go onto bigger and better aircraft, culminating in our experiences in the Lancaster.

A vital part of our training involved dinghy drills, consisting of practising escaping from a downed aircraft which had ditched in the sea and struggling into the aircraft's dinghy. Many a badly-damaged aircraft had given up the fight on the return flight over the North Sea and had plummeted down to land in a welter of spray on a cold, unforgiving surface.

If they were lucky they were picked up fairly quickly by the Walrus aircraft or fast launches of the Air-Sea Rescue Service, if not, as too often happened, they found a cold, lonely death waiting for them. Thankfully, I never had the need to blow the emergency whistle we all carried stitched on our battledress collar in anger!

We flew cross-country missions, all the while learning of the superb handling qualities of the Stirling. I learned alongside the others, seated at my table in the cramped fuselage and occupying my time in the air with the myriad tasks a WOP/AG would confront. Practising Morse at every opportunity, I became ultra-proficient, listening out for our call sign and the messages that passed between aircraft and the ground. Harry Brooker continued to lead us, his unflappable character and imperturbability soothing fractious nerves as he flung the aircraft through a series of difficult manoeuvres without a hint of nerves.

Incidents abounded during this phase of our training such as the navigator who chased his flight bag into a whirling propeller and the sorrow felt for friends lost in flying accidents of all causes. All the while, I found myself withdrawing from close relationships, the very nature of the training causing me to retreat further into myself in order to avoid the pain caused by the *loss of a good friend. The members of my own crew became my closest companions, each adding their own components to the relationship.'*

Recognising the threat posed by a resurgent Germany, in 1936 the British Air Ministry issued a specification for a twin-engined medium bomber. Named the Avro Manchester it first flew in mid-1939, entering service with the RAF in November 1940. Broadly speaking, the aircraft was an operational disaster, compounded in no small way by the use of the Rolls-Royce Vulture engine. The engine proved to be horrifically unreliable with the result that an onboard failure of one in the air meant the aircraft was unable to sustain flight, all too often with disastrous results. Eventually, after an unacceptable loss rate on operations, the Manchester was withdrawn in 1942.

Enter the might Lancaster, or 'Lanc' as she was affectionately known. Sixty-nine feet long and over nineteen feet high the aircraft was enormous, becoming the most famous and most widely-utilised of all the British bombers of World War Two. The Lancaster and the throb of its four Rolls-Royce Merlin engines became the most familiar sight and sound over mainland Britain during the war, its enormous lifting capacity and cavernous 33ft long bomb-bay enabling it to carry the 4,000lb 'cookie' blast bomb and after modification the 8,000lb 'cookie', the 12,000lb 'Tallboy' and the 22,000lb aptly-named, 'Grand Slam'.

The aircraft's designer, Ray Chadwick, took the existing Manchester airframe and added four Merlins to replace the two Vultures. The triple tail fin was disposed of and two elliptical fins fitted in their place. After a few modifications, none major, the aircraft was flown and found to be inherently stable, a great pilot's aircraft. Over 7,000 Lancasters were manufactured during the war, a fitting testimony to the aircraft's operational qualities.

During the course of operations more than 3,000 Lancasters were lost in action but thirty-five would reach or surpass 100 operations, three of these survivors flying with 61 Squadron.

The Lancaster usually flew with a crew of seven. In the nose, lying prone was the bomb-aimer who also manned a twin .303 Browning machine-gun equipped turret. In the spacious cockpit, sat on the left was the aircraft's pilot with his blind-flying panel of instruments and gauges. Seated next to him on a less comfortable seat was the flight engineer whose job it was to monitor the aircraft's systems and fuel consumption, as well as acting as a back-up pilot if required.

Immediately behind the cockpit, on the left-hand side of the fuselage, was the small, cramped workspace laid out for the navigator and further aft of him sat the wireless operator and his sets. Many navigators preferred to draw the curtain and work from behind its security, never venturing out from take-off to landing. From his table he would work out the aircraft and the target's position from their navigational equipment or star-shots when necessary, allowing the pilot to fly to and from the target on the most economical route.

With the astrodome above him and the warm air heating outlet alongside his station, the wireless operator could claim to be the most comfortable of the crew. He could also be the most unpopular as it was he who controlled the cabin heating and it was he who bore the brunt of his crew's displeasure if they thought the temperature was too low.

Besides listening out for Group and Base instructions, another duty of the wireless operator, not often discussed, was his part in summoning help should the aircraft have to ditch. It was Leslie who would be relied upon to tap out their final position before scrambling to join his comrades in exiting the doomed aircraft

Aft of his workspace was the wings main spar spanning the width of the fuselage, over which the forward crew members had to squeeze to reach their position in the front of the aircraft. The final two crew positions were those of the mid-upper and tail gunner. The mid-upper gunner manned a twin .303 Browning-equipped turret whilst the tail gunner's lonely position at the extreme rear of the aircraft held the sting in the tail, four .303 Brownings in twin mounts. These last two crew members wore electrically-heated suits as the fuselage aft of the armoured door was not heated.

At the very rear of the fuselage was situated a primitive Elsan toilet, the portable unit being designed to give them somewhere to relieve themselves during the long flights over enemy territory. The complexities of trying to undo heavy flying clothing combined with the freezing temperatures at high altitudes discouraged many from using the Elsan and most aircrew tried to adjust their food intake before a flight so as not to require its services.

Here are a few facts and figures about the Avro Lancaster and the costs that went into ensuring each single aircraft was ready before taking off to complete an operation:

Each Lancaster cost £42,000 to purchase from the manufacturer.

Each aircraft required the use of 5,000 tons of aluminium to build.

Each aircraft carried the equivalent radio and radar equipment to fabricate 1,000,000 domestic radios of the period.

Each aircraft absorbed the equivalent manhours required to build one mile of a modern highway.

Each member of a Lancaster crew cost £10,000 to train, making each aircraft worth £112,000 or £122,000 if an eighth crew member was carried.

To fuel, bomb and arm a Lancaster required an additional £13,000, taking into account the cost of training ground crews.

This made the cost to the economy for every <u>single</u> Lancaster lost on a sortie approximately £135,000.

In view of the losses of Lancasters through the autumn of 1943 and the winter of 1943/44, including severe losses incurred during the Battle of Berlin, the War Office decided that heavy bomber crews would carry out their training on the Halifax and Stirling, leaving the Lancaster to be operated by front-line squadrons only. After completing their operational training the crews would then carry out a conversion course onto the Lancaster before being passed ready for operations.

Statistically, a Lancaster crew were in far more danger when trying to evacuate a crippled aircraft in the air than, say, a Halifax by virtue of the Lancaster's smaller, tighter escape hatches which hindered an easy egress. Compound that with the tension and terror of men struggling under immense mental strain as they attempted to escape and it becomes obvious how difficult such an operation could be when carried out at night, often on fire and with an aircraft falling and skidding headlong out of the skies.

A farsighted officer, Group Captain Peter Johnson DSO DFC AFC and a future CO of 97 Squadron, initiated a programme of training Lancaster crews in how to carry out such an arduous task. As the CO of RAF Syerston, the Lancaster Finishing School, he obtained several Lancaster fuselages from aircraft due to be scrapped and blacked out any light inside that might aid the trainees. Crews were then taught their dinghy and escape drill under conditions that were at the time as realistic as possible, a factor that helped many aircrew in the future who found themselves attempting the real thing when their aircraft were shot down.

Accordingly, in May 1944 Harry Brooker and his crew were posted to 51 Base and arrived at RAF Syerston to begin their conversion onto the Lancaster. For the next few weeks they flew in different weather conditions as they became used to the aircraft's capabilities and forgiving nature. For a pilot she was a dream to handle and her sturdy construction gave all of them increased confidence for when the day came that they'd leave to begin operations.

'It was to Lancasters that the 'Brooker Crew' as we called ourselves were posted and a Heavy Conversion Course was necessary to enable us to become used to the aircraft before venturing out over Europe on operations. It was a decision we'd come to appreciate over the coming months as our experience grew and the number of successful raids we participated in increased.

Our first look at the type of aircraft we would fly all our operations in filled us with awe. 69ft long and rising off the ground to a height of 19ft, her service ceiling was in excess of 23,000ft. Resting on her huge tyres, nose pointing skywards, the Lancaster looked the part she was to play from 1942 onwards, that of the best and hardest-hitting bomber of all time.

We took no time in assuming our positions in the aircraft and so began the final phase of our training. Any apprehension soon disappeared as the flying qualities of the aircraft became apparent, elation taking over from nervousness as Harry Brooker tested the aircraft to its limits in order to discover what it was capable of. We took several weeks between May and July to complete our training but succeeded and finally arrived on the morning of the 24th July 1944 at

RAF Skellingthorpe in Lincolnshire to join 61 Squadron and begin our tour.

I was particularly pleased with the aircraft. I had the warmest seat in the house, being next to the heater output, and suffered a lot of good-natured banter from the rest of the crew over my being able to keep warm whilst they froze.

Like a lot of other crews, we tended to keep to ourselves, socialising off the base with a few quiet beers and only really meeting up with the other aircrew at briefings or social events on the base itself. With the continuing losses in men and machines, it didn't pay to become too close with other airmen from outside your own circle. With one's fate being tied up with the other six men you flew with it was to these that you looked to for companionship, nothing else seemed to matter.'

RAF Skellingthorpe, located four miles South-west of the city of Lincoln and just two miles from the village of Skellingthorpe opened as a bomber base in 1941, housing Hampdens and Manchester squadrons before her runways were extended in June 1942 to accommodate the Lancasters of 50 Squadron and 61 Squadron. 61 Squadron with her sixteen aircraft arrived there in November of 1943. Skellingthorpe's losses during the war were 208, comprising of 15 Hampdens, 6 Manchesters and 187 Lancasters.

According to many aircrew the base was a complete shambles, with a long walk between the Nissen huts, which provided accommodation, to the nearest ablutions and the Sergeant's Mess. The huts were heated by a coke-burning stove that failed to provide sufficient heat, making for freezing conditions in the dead of winter. Being low-lying the huts gathered water in the winter, icy water flowing in one door and out the other, making it a miserable existence for tired crews fresh off an overnight raid

At the start of the war, 61 Squadron was based at Hemswell, flying Hampdens. It had a lot of Polish aircrew and it was noticed that whilst squadron orders were to bring bombs back if crews couldn't find the target, the Polish crews never returned with bombs onboard. When asked why they always managed to find the target they replied simply, '*All* of Germany is the target!'

61 Squadron's Operations log for the month of July 1944 notes the arrival of: *132791 F/O H.Brooker, Pilot, from 51 Base to 61 Squadron with effect from 24/7/44.*

A month earlier on 6th June 160,000 allied troops stormed ashore on the beaches of Normandy along a 50-mile front. Years in the planning, the landings took the Germans by surprise and fierce fighting took place as the allies fought to gain a foothold. Prior to the great day Bomber Command's campaign against Germany had been halted and instead crews were sent during both day and night to bomb targets in France, railway marshalling yards, troop barracks and fuel depots. 61 Squadron played its part in these attacks but it was the growing V1 menace that Harry Brooker's crew would confront soon after their arrival at Skellingthorpe.

Chapter Three

Before continuing with Leslie's story, let us stop and take stock of the conduct of the air war as Harry Brooker's crew began their tour of operations.

At the start of the war there was no standard method of determining the success or failure of bombing missions, the RAF simply relied on the words of crews as to whether or not they had successfully reached and bombed their designated target. To assist in collating intelligence reports on the veracity of the crew's assertions, Bomber Command began fitting cameras to bombers in 1941. On pressing the bomb release a photo-flash would operate seconds after the bombs fell away, taking a picture of the ground beneath the attacking aircraft and giving an indication of the bombs trajectory to the target.

Lord Cherwell, the Chief Scientific Advisor to the Cabinet instigated a report which compared several hundred of these photographs taken over the target to the claims of the aircrews. Known as 'The Butt Report', named after the civil servant given the task of investigating these claims, the document was circulated in August of 1941 and shocked many in the echelons of Bomber Command and the government.

Simply put, the Butt Report damned the crew's claims by reporting that of those photographs studied, only one in three aircraft who recorded attacking the target actually bombed within five miles of the target. Over the industrial heart of Germany known as the 'Ruhr', it was only one in ten. Taken as an overall percentage it appeared that only five per cent of bombers attacking a target bombed within five miles of that target.

The recriminations were immediate. Other reports were commissioned to try and water down the impact of the Butt Report and in early 1942 Lord Cherwell produced a paper which postulated the idea of abandoning the concept of precision bombing then practiced by Bomber Command and switching to one of area bombing. By swamping the target with hundreds of aircraft they could overwhelm the target's defences and cause maximum damage over a wide area.

A week after the area bombing directive was published in February 1942, a small, dapper Air Marshall assumed his post of Air Officer Commanding Bomber Command. Arthur Travers 'Bomber' Harris and the bombing campaign over Occupied Europe were from then on to be forever linked.

Sometimes known as 'Butcher' Harris or just plain 'Butch', Arthur Harris served in the Great War as a pilot on the Western front. He stayed in the RAF after the Armistice and continued to rise steadily in rank, serving in the Middle East and at the start of World War Two was an Air-Vice Marshall commanding 5 Group in Lincolnshire. Promoted to Air Marshall in 1941 he assumed the title of Commander-in-Chief of Bomber Command in 1942 and energetically began to rectify the deficiencies he saw in the men and units he now commanded.

Loved by most, hated by more than a few, Harris was an uncompromising figure who saw his role as that of carrying out the job of reducing Germany's ability to wage war. To do that meant the systematic destruction of her industries and the cities and towns that housed those industries. De-housing the workers engaged in these activities would cause massive disruption to the German war effort and it was on the advent of this campaign that Harris uttered his famous words: *'They sowed the wind and now they shall reap the whirlwind.'* It should not be forgotten at this stage of the war that the bombing campaign he instigated was the only option for direct confrontation with Germany and that for four years of the war the only way to confront Germany militarily in Europe was by the use of the aircraft and men of Bomber Command.

Thus, whilst Leslie and his fellow trainees continued in their efforts to reach operational status, from 1942 onwards Harris sent increasingly-larger forces against the heavily-defended cities of Germany. As more of the 'Heavies' such as the Halifax and Lancaster reached the front-line squadrons, they were added to the vast fleets taking to the skies on favourable nights.

The port of Lübeck could be said to be the recipient of the first air raid aimed purely at the German population and not at industrial targets. On the night of the 28th March 1942, 400 tons of bombs and 25,000 incendiaries rained down on the town from 234 aircraft, causing extensive damage to large areas of the mainly wooden houses. RAF losses were 12 aircraft.

On 30/31st May 1942, the city of Cologne suffered from the efforts of the first-ever 1,000 bomber raid. Scraped together from Bomber, and Flying Training Command the aircraft devastated large swathes of the city. New tactics of a bomber stream which flew along a common route were introduced for this raid and different heights were allotted to different aircraft types. The new navigational aid of 'GEE' was utilised to ensure more precise navigation and reduce the risk of mid-air collisions. Essen and Bremen soon felt the weight of similar attacks and the frantic Germans were forced to switch a major part of their war industry to the production of anti-aircraft guns and a massive reorganisation of the *Luftwaffe's* night-fighter force.

GEE was a radar navigational aid which replaced the dead reckoning and occasional radio bearing 'fix' method of locating targets. By receiving a set of radio pulses from Britain, a bomber could calculate its position and follow a set course to its target whatever the weather. The one drawback was its range, approximately 350 miles but it was easy to operate and gave great hope to the High

Command that at last a safe, reliable method of finding targets at night had now been discovered.

RAF casualties on the Cologne raid were comparatively light given the number of aircraft involved, 41 aircraft lost, the majority being twin-engined Wellingtons with only one Lancaster out of the 87 deployed being lost. This was the highest total loss for a raid up until then but given the number of aircraft involved, the loss rate of 3.9% was deemed to be acceptable. Most of the losses were put down to the perfect weather over the target which not only helped ensure the success of the bombing but also greatly aided the German defences.

Over the next two years Germany would be devastated by larger and longer air raids, flattening huge areas of her towns and cities. Raids on Hamburg in July/August of 1943 brought with them the horrifying phenomenon of the 'firestorm'. Specific weather over the target led to the creation of fierce winds that rushed in to fill the vacuum left by the oxygen consumed by the incendiary bombs dropped by the attacking aircraft. The resulting high temperatures melted tarmac in the streets and immolated thousands of Hamburg's inhabitants, an estimated total of 43,000 people losing their lives.

Harris launched the 'Battle of Berlin' in November of 1943, quoting; *'It will cost 400-500 aircraft but will cost Germany the war.'* In the event, the battle for the 'Big City' as it was known would cost the allies over 1,200 aircraft in direct raids on the city and other supporting raids. On the night of 16/17th December 1943, for example, 51 Lancasters were lost, 25 over the target and 29 on landing back in Britain in bad weather. Three nights later on the 20/21st December, 27 Halifax's and 14 Lancasters were lost over Berlin, many to nightfighters.

The four-month long battle cost the RAF 500 aircraft lost over the city, with 2,690 aircrew killed and another 1,000 ending up as POW's. For Bomber Command and its crews, this failure to force Germany out of the war meant the conflict would rage for another sixteen months. Berlin was at the operational limit of the RAF's capabilities, a long flight outward and inward with tired crews battling all the way to the target and back against the elements and the German defences.

Berlin was out of effective GEE range but in early 1943 another new airborne radar aid was making its mark. H2S used a rotating dish placed underneath its parent aircraft to map the ground below on a Plan Position Indicator (PPI) for the navigator to interpret. This not only enabled navigation to the target in cloud but allowed precise bombing attacks to be carried out. Berlin, with its many lakes clearly visible on the PPI, enabled a more accurate pattern of bombs to be achieved.

In spite of all these aids, Bomber Command losses would begin to mount following the increased raids on Germany as the German's nightfighter force became more proficient and the flak barrages surrounding key areas were improved. In the first twelve months of the war, the RAF lost 342 aircraft with 1,381 aircrew killed, 175 of those aircraft lost by daylight sorties. By 1942 the losses had increased to another 914 aircraft, of which 421 were claimed by the nascent nightfighter force (Compared with only 42 in 1940!)

By September of 1942 over 15,000 aircrew had been killed, wounded or were prisoners of war with another 5,000 killed or wounded in training accidents. From April 1943 to October 1944, 2,703 aircraft failed to return from bombing sorties with the loss of 19,000 aircrew, most of them to nightfighters who claimed over 1,000 victories between November 1943 to March 1944. The night sky was becoming an increasingly dangerous medium to operate in as the nightfighter strength grew and the flak defences improved.

As the bomber offensive against Germany intensified, the *Luftwaffe's* response had been as haphazard as the RAF's attempts to locate its targets. German fighter aircraft took to the skies to seek out their prey in an uncoordinated manner, simply wandering the skies until they found a bomber to engage. In June 1940 the first dedicated nightfighter unit was established and months later the appointment of a *Luftwaffe* officer would make the skies that much more dangerous for the bomber stream known to the Germans as *'Der Dicke Hund'*, 'The Fat Dog.'

In October 1940, *Generaloberst* Josef Kammhuber was ordered to reform the nascent nightfighter force and applied himself with a vengeance to the task. His involvement led to the formation of the 'Kammhuber Line', a defensive system that stretched from Denmark to France. New radar systems were introduced and began to gain positive results. The first, 'FREYA', was a long-range radar system that detected the bomber stream as it formed over the English coastline and headed for Europe.

Europe was split into defined areas known as 'boxes' into which the attacking nightfighter would be managed by the instructions from two 'WÜRZBURG' shorter-range radar units. The nightfighters would take off from their airbase as 'FREYA' alerted the German defenders to an incoming raid and orbit a radio beacon, waiting until the ground controller issued instructions as an enemy bomber entered the 'box'. They would then close with the bomber and engage it as their own air-borne radar set picked up the returns from the bomber. One Würzburg would then track the bomber and the other would track the fighter.

The main method of attack was to slide in from behind and try to fly, unseen, beneath the bomber. The nightfighter pilot would then pull up, almost to the point of stalling, and fire a short burst into the belly and wings of the bomber before peeling away and diving out of range.

Between ten and fifteen 20mm cannon rounds were usually suffice to set the bomber's wing-mounted fuel tanks on fire and the aircraft was doomed from then on.

This method of attack carried with it a high risk to the nightfighter and it was a serving nightfighter pilot and his ground-crew armourer who came up with a novel solution. Oberleutnant Rudolf Schonert and his corporal, Paul Mahle fitted two 20mm cannon mounted behind the cockpit of Schonert's Me110 nightfighter.

The guns were positioned to fire upwards at an angle of around 78° to the vertical and the fighter could then slide in using a classic attack mode that became known as *'Von hinten unten'* (From behind and below.), pouring its fire into the bomber from a more stable flight attitude. The Germans called this method of utilising cannon mounted in this way as *'Schräge Musik'*, or 'Jazz Music' from the sound of the cannons firing.

'Schräge Musik' came into use around the time of the Peenemunde raid of August 1943, when combats using this method became more and more frequent and large scores were rattled up by *Luftwaffe* pilots willing to close in and take the risks of close-quarter fighting in this manner. *Major* Heinz-Wolfgang Schnaufer (121 victories.). *Oberst* Helmut Lent (110 victories.) and *Major* Heinrich Prinz zu Sayn Wittgenstein (83 victories.) all shot down large numbers of RAF bombers and multiple claims per night became the norm.

The new method dispensed with the use of tracer and the first a bomber crew knew they were under attack was when the cannon shells passed through or exploded inside their aircraft. It was estimated that from August 1943 until the end of the war in May 1945, four out of every five RAF bombers downed were shot down using the *'Schrage Musik'* method of attack.

Many bomber crews informed the Intelligence Officers at briefing on their return from an 'op' of the strange fireballs seen in the sky. They were reassured by being told this was a new type of airborne flare the Germans were using, known as 'Scarecrows' and was an attempt by the Germans into fooling them that they had just witnessed one of their own aircraft blowing up in mid-air. It was not until after the war that it became widely known that the Germans had never possessed anything of the sort and that what the crews had seen were in fact aircraft being destroyed in a *Schräge Musik* tracer-less attack.

The overall method of attacking by radar guidance at night became known as *Zähme Sau* or, 'Tame Boar.' In July 1943, the RAF attacked Hamburg in Northern Germany and used 'Window' for the first time in an attempt to confuse the enemy radar. 'Window' was thin strips of aluminium cut to one half of the target radar's wavelength which swamped the enemy radar screens with multiple returns. One bundle per minute was dropped through the flare-chute and the resulting 'snowstorm' blinded the Freya and Würzburg radars, with losses involving this method dropping dramatically.

The *Luftwaffe's* response was to develop another attack method known as *'Wilde Sau'*, 'Wild boar', whereby single-seater fighters as well as nightfighters roamed the skies by night and day. These aircraft searched for the bomber stream with the aid of a higher concentration of searchlights in the target area but without the use of radar guidance. This was not as successful but nevertheless, significant losses were sustained by the bomber streams. The new nightfighter radar introduced in early 1944, *Lichtenstein* SN2, was not confused by 'Window' at the time of its introduction so airborne acquisition of targets was still possible.

The German flak defences were also tightened up at this time, belts of anti-aircraft guns being laid out in the most common approach routes of the bombers, as well as encircling German towns and cities. Using the feared

88mm gun and its 20lb shell, they could throw up a radar-predicted barrage at the bomber stream's altitude and heading, forcing them to fly through a maelstrom of flame and white-hot metal. The use of powerful searchlights aided in locating the bombers, particularly the blue master beams that the aircrews came to fear. It was all a matter of luck and fate when passing overhead, on a good day you flew safely through the barrage, on a bad day you were damaged or were shot down, it was as simple as that.

On the night of 30/31st March 1944, a force of 782 aircraft took off to bomb the German town of Nuremburg. Before the night ended, a total of 105 aircraft would be lost, 64 Lancasters and 31 Halifaxes on the operation itself whilst 10 aircraft crashed on landing in Britain, a crippling loss rate of 13.6%. Almost 900 aircrew were dead, wounded, or prisoners-of-war. German losses were 10 nightfighters. It was a night when the weather was clear, the time flying over Germany was too long and bomber stream flew in too straight a line, giving the nightfighters equipped with SN2 and *'Schräge Musik'* plenty of time to acquire their targets.

To help them in their defence against the nightfighters, RAF aircraft began carrying a new type of tail-mounted radar warning device. Known as 'MONICA' it warned an aircraft of an enemy's approach and enabled them to take defensive measures such as 'corkscrewing', a violent and twisting airborne manoeuvre to evade the fighter. After examining a shot-down Lancaster fitted with this equipment, the Germans developed 'FLENSBURG' which in turn homed in on the 'MONICA' emissions. 'NAXOS' was also developed at the same time to detect the bomber's *H2S* transmissions. These measures and counter-measures were to be an increasing technological part of the war as Harry Brooker's crew drew up to the gates of Skellingthorpe to join the Lancasters of 61 Squadron.

Leslie's initial thoughts were mixed as they arrived at their new station:

'It was from here we'd be taking off on our first operational mission as a trained crew and the tension was already apparent as we were greeted and allocated billets The station was a mess, deep mud surrounded all the billets and the Airman's Mess where we were to eat was a long walk away. A more dispiriting start to operations could not be envisaged.'

The rank structure of a Bomber Command base was as follows:
Station Commander was a Group Captain.
Squadron Commander was a Wing Commander.
Flight Commander was a Squadron leader.
Deputy Flight Commander was a Flight Lieutenant. (8 aircraft per Flight.)

61 Squadron had formed at Hemswell in Lincolnshire in 1937, its motto being "*Per purum tonantes*", which translates as "Thundering through the clear air." and the squadron badge being The Lincoln Imp. Based at Skellingthorpe from April 1944 inwards, Flt Lt William 'Bill' Reid was to win the Victoria Cross in 1943 with 61 Sqn in November 1943. The squadron flew more operations with the Lancaster than any other in the RAF and ended up as having completed the second highest total of operations on heavy bombers in the war.

The Lancaster carried a variety of bomb loads intended for specific targets and those listed below would have been carried by 61 Squadron aircraft:

<u>'Arson.'</u> Area Bombing Raids (Maximum Incendiary.) 14 Small Bomb Containers (SBC) each loaded with 236x4lb

No.16 Incendiary and No.15x Explosive Incendiary (1 in 10 mix) bombs. Total bomb load 14,000lbs.
Target Type: General.
'Abnormal.' Area Bombing raids (Industrial Demolition). 14x1,000lb Medium Case(MC) General Purpose (GP) RDX or US short-finned High Explosive(HE) bombs. With mix of instantaneous (Nose-armed) and long-delay (Up to 144 hours, tail-armed) fusing.
Target Type: Factories, Rail Yards, Dockyards.
'Cookie/Plumduff.' Area Bombing Raids (Blast, Fire and Demolition.) 1x4,000lb Amatol, Minol or Tritonal-filled, impact fused High Capacity (HC) bomb, 3x1,000lb short-finned, short-delay, tail-armed HE bombs, and up to 6SBC's with 4lb or 30lb incendiary bombs.
Target Type: Heavily industrialised cities.
'Plumduff-Plus.' Area Bombing Raids (Blast and Demolition.) 1xMk.1or Mk.II 8,000lbs HC containing 6,361lbs of Amatex, with barometric or impact fuse and up to 6x500lbs MC or GP bombs with instantaneous or long-delay fusing.
Target Type: Heavily industrialised cities.
'Usual.' Area Bombing Raids (Blast and Maximum Incendiary.) 1x4,000lb impact-fused HC bomb (Cookie) and 12 SBC's each loaded with either 25x30lb or 236x4lb No.15 or 15x incendiary bombs.
Target Type: General. (Most common bomb-load carried by the Lancaster.)
'No-Ball.' Carpet-Bombing of Tactical Targets (V1 Sites.) 1x4,000lb HC impact-fused bomb (Cookie) and up to 18x500lb MC or GP bombs, short-finned with mixed instantaneous and delay fusing.
Target Type: V1 sites, radar sites, armour concentrations.

The 12,000lb 'Tallboy' and 22,000lb 'Grand Slam' bombs, both designed by Barnes Wallis of Dambuster fame, were only carried in the specially-modified Lancasters operated by 617 Squadron.

The 4,000lb 'cookie' as it was known was a thin-cased projectile filled with Amatol and designed to take the roofs off buildings so that the accompanying incendiaries that were dropped with it could set fire to the interiors. Shaped like a dustbin, it had all the aerodynamic qualities of one and was a dangerous beast to carry as the detonators were notoriously unpredictable.

'Before we flew together on our first 'op', Harry Brooker flew as a 'second dickey' with an experienced crew. On the night of the 24/25th July he flew with P/O Watkins and his crew in their Lancaster Mk.1-ME595, squadron registration QR-Y on a raid to the oil refinery and storage depot at Donges, near the mouth of the River Loire in France. They encountered many searchlights and lots of light flak but few fighters were seen, a sobering introduction to the night war for Harry Brooker. This was a common way to allow a pilot new to operations to experience how a crew came together in the air and Harry flew in the cramped Flight Engineer's seat, with the Flight Engineer standing behind him. The flight passed with no encountered problems and Harry Brooker was then classified as ready to fly on operations with his own crew.'

The following entry comes from 61 Sqn's Operations Log for the 24/25th July 1944: **Attack on Donges.** *Lancaster ME595 QR-Y.F/O H.Watkins(Pilot), Sgt P.W.Jowitt(Flt Eng), F/S D.J.Hockin(Nav), Sgt W.E.Ray(Bomb Aimer), P/O M.J.Ware(WOP/AG), Sgt K.A. Johnston(M/Upper), F/Sgt C.J. Foy(Rear Gunner), F/O H.Brooker (2nd Pilot). Up 2228 down 0359. F/O Watkins considered the defences rather heavy, many searchlights with a lot of light flak, no fighters were observed. A large explosion was seen at 0146hrs followed by a column of thick black* smoke. *Another explosion was also seen at 0149hrs. Bombed Green T.I (Target Indicator.) as ordered from 9,5000ft at 0147hrs. PHOTO. Ground detail.*

Contrast that fairly uneventful operation to the drama awaiting Watkins and his crew the very next evening. The 61 Sqn Operations Log entry reads: 25th July 1944: **Attack on St Cyr.** *Lancaster LM481 QR-0. Up 1736 down 2200. F/O Watkins states very good trip to target. In target area, 11,000ft hit by falling bombs from Lancaster a/c. Rear turret carried away, starboard wing tip damaged.* **Rear gunner also carried away and presumed killed.** *Target area clear. Running up just before bombing received warning from Mid Upper Gunner that plane converging just above, held aircraft for bombs and photograph. Bombing height 11,000ft. 1957hrs. Aiming point 'B'. PHOTO. Ground detail.*

P/O Watkins' Lancaster LM481, QR-O, was struck at 11,000ft over the target of St Cyr by three bombs dropped from another aircraft above. Their aircraft was badly damaged with the entire rear turret being carried away together with the starboard rudder and tail-fin and a large part of the starboard wing tip. The rear gunner, F/Sgt C.J.Foy was killed and is buried in the Commonwealth War Graves Cemetery in Fontenay-le-Fleary, Versailles, France.

Harold Watkins managed to fly his crippled aircraft back to England where he made an emergency landing at RAF Wickenby, near Lincoln. Incredibly, showing great fortitude, Harold Watkins and his crew flew the very next evening on an operation to Givors, albeit with a new aircraft and rear gunner, Sgt D.Copson. As for Harry Brooker, he was given just one day to come to terms with the shocking death of someone he'd flown with the previous night before being informed that he would be taking his own aircraft and crew on operations.

The great day dawned on 26th July, 1944. After a brief airtest the nervous and all too self-conscious crew gathered with the other crews in the Briefing Room to discover where they would be flying on their very first operation. Their first operation was to be a night raid operation against the railway yards at Givors, France. The expected weather en-route was explained and noted, routes worked out to and from the target. Identifications, heights, type of bomb load carried; take-off time, place in the formation, Bomb Aimers preview,

Navigator's settings, GEE coordinates, IFF (Identification Friend or Foe) switch on/off, fuel logistics, W/OP's briefing, codes, signals, logging, all this information was hurled at them at lightning and bewildering speed to be rapidly assimilated and stored in the recesses of their minds.

The gunners were given the disposition of the enemy fighter force in the area to be attacked, locations of known anti-aircraft belts and searchlights and made their preparations accordingly. Other details were crammed into the recesses of Leslie's mind; when and where they were to throw 'Window' from the flare chute, the contents of the aircraft's bomb-bay and photo-cell placement for the bomb-release camera should it be needed.

Dismissed from the briefing they stumbled back to their billets to contemplate the time left to them before take-off. A meal, already organised, was well received and they ate hungrily like gladiators awaiting their call to the arena. Some smoked incessantly, glanced frequently at their watches while gazing blankly into space whilst others wrote furiously to relatives and loved ones. All the months of training had come down to this, the agonising wait until the time came to report to the flight-line and board their aircraft.

Time passed all too quickly. Pulling on fleece-lined flying boots and sporting white woollen pullovers under battledress tunics they were called to the dispersal area where they collected their parachutes and struggled into the bulky sets of flying clothing and Irvine Jackets. Filled vacuum flasks were placed into their flight bags and Benzedrine tablets packed alongside chocolate bars and escape kits. The tablets were to be taken to help keep them awake in the air but many aircrews scorned the use of them. Pre-flight checks completed, Harry Brooker signed the all important A700 form and the crew boarded their aircraft, a Lancaster III QR-I, stomachs churning, to prepare for take-off.

A final look around as they climbed the short ladder at the rear of the aircraft and they were ready. The rear gunner and mid-upper manned their turrets at the rear as the rest of the crew passed through the armoured door forward of the mid-upper's position and locked the door. Each man took up his position in the metal cocoon and waited tensely.

Heart pounding, Leslie squirmed over the main spar and placed his parachute in its stowage next to his seat before seating himself and switching on his two radio sets, the R1155 Receiver which sat on top of the T1154 Transmitter. As they warmed up he made his first-ever operational entry into his radio logbook, glancing out through the fuselage window onto the port engine. Mentally uttering a short prayer to God for their safe return he listened as the crew responded to Harry Brooker's voice carrying out an intercom check, everyone reporting their position in the aircraft and reassuring him that they were ready to go. A loud explosion of sound informed them all of the first engine starting up and the tension increased.

When all four engines had been started and checked, permission was asked and received to take their place in the queue for take-off. The chocks were removed, the brakes released and with a shimmy and a lurch, the

Lancaster rolled slowly but smoothly from her position on the dispersal as the throttles were opened. Moving ponderously, she headed towards the perimeter track before swinging onto the runway. Crossing himself as they swung round, Leslie waited anxiously for the engine note to increase as they headed down the runway when... Disaster.

Judicial use of the throttles was crucial to the Lancaster's ability to turn, the pilot having to judge very finely when to open the required outboard engine's throttle to swing them to the left or right. As the Lancaster slewed round to line up it overran the tarmac, strayed onto the grass and struck a post protruding eighteen inches out of the ground, puncturing the port main wheel. The crew were aware of a loud *thud!* Followed by even louder imprecations as Harry Brooker informed the Control Tower of his aircraft's plight.

With fine timings involved for the raid, there was no time to repair the aircraft and get them airborne and no spare aircraft to transfer into. Disappointment was mixed with a guilty feeling of relief and a chastened crew abandoned the aircraft to anxiously await the squadron's return as the rest of the aircraft accelerated down the runway and disappeared into the sky. The 'Lincoln Imp' (61 Sqn's badge.) was smiling on them that night as the squadron returned without loss and they mixed with the returning crews to hear their stories and have their legs pulled over aborting their very first 'op'.

They were to miss the next raid, against Stuttgart, on the night of 28/29th July. 61 Squadron put up 16 aircraft that night but over France, in clear skies, the German nightfighters fell on the Main Force and 36 Lancasters were lost. One of those aircraft lost was a 61 Sqn Lancaster, QR-T, LM452 piloted by F/Sgt W.R.Macpherson which was shot down with only one survivor. Two men escaped the burning aircraft but whilst the bomb-aimer, Sgt R.G.McMillan RCAF landed and was taken captive, the navigator, Sgt P.P. Brosko RCAF was captured and murdered. A grim welcome to operations for Leslie and his friends.

It would appear that Sgt Peter Paul Brosko was handed over to the *Luftwaffe* soon after landing and was taken out and shot. Post-war, the men responsible were apprehended, tried and sentenced to death for war crimes. The junior ranks were hanged but the senior German officer, one Frederick Kramer, was shot by firing squad.

'Any euphoria we might have felt at not coming to grief on our first operational take-off was soon dismissed as, after several days of lengthy cross-country flights, we were once again entombed within a Lancaster I, QR-R. This time we were preparing for an evening raid on the railway marshalling yards near the village of Joigny-Laroche, ninety miles southeast of Paris.

'Tail gunner?'

'Present, skipper.' A laconic answer from the rear.

'Mid-upper?'

'Here, skipper.'

Calmly, Harry Brooker went through the rest of the crew positions, gaining a positive answer for each of his queries. Satisfied that we were all onboard and ready, Harry signalled to the waiting ground crew looking up at his open side window. A trolley accumulator supplied the ground power, saving the need to use the aircraft's batteries. It also saved Bill Morgan the Flight Engineer having to climb onto the wings and prime each engine's fuel pump manually in turn.

'Ok, chaps, starting port outer.'

He signalled to the ground 'erk' and pressed the starter button. With a piercing whine the port outer prop began to revolve slowly, picking up speed. A loud cough sounded and a brief burst of orange flame lit up from the exhaust stubs as the fuel in the cylinders ignited and the Merlin engine's revolutions increased. The noise settled down to a steady roar and Harry Brooker deftly started the remaining engines, the port inner next, starboard inner and last of all, the starboard outer.

Sat on his right, Bill Morgan studied his instruments intently, ensuring that the hydraulics were operational and that each engine's fuel supplies were switched on and functioning normally. He checked that the crossfeed system was switched off, booster pumps 'on', selected the right fuel tank and raised his hand, thumb up, and Harry acknowledged this with a nod of his head.

Signalling for the chocks to be removed he made his pre-taxi checks before a terse transmission to the Tower gave him by return, permission to taxi out to take our place in the long line of aircraft waiting to swing onto the runway. For those strapped into their positions in the aircraft, this took an age but at long last a heavily-laden QR-R lined up on the runway and waited, wings quivering. Settling himself in his seat, Harry Brooker carried out the all-important take-off checks. Gyro, trim, radiator cooling gills, mixture, fuel and, lastly, flaps set to their take-off position of 15°. Satisfied all was in order, he smoothly advanced the throttles as a green Aldis lamp flashed briefly from the control van.

'Here we go.' At his words, everyone tensed, waiting for the aircraft to begin her rollout. The gunners, bomb-aimer and pilot's positions afforded them a grandstand view of the take-off but for Ken Brown and myself, the navigator and wireless operator seated at our cramped tables, the take-off was a blur of *deafening noise and vibration that hid our fears as we willed QR-R to become airborne.*

With the brakes released the aircraft began to accelerate down the tarmac strip. Faster and faster she went, with Harry Brooker's left hand lightly gripping the control column as he used the port throttle and rudders to counter the natural swing to port caused by the massive torque from the propellers all turning in the same direction. With Bill Morgan's hands now clamped firmly over the throttles, Harry watched his airspeed gradually build up. The Lancaster began to rise naturally as the airflow over her wings increased but he kept her level, pushing on the control column to lift the tail off the ground until the required speed was achieved and he gently eased back on the controls.

She rose easily, dipped for a brief second then began climbing and turning steadily into the beckoning sky. A loud thump indicated the undercarriage had retracted safely and all on board breathed a little easier. Shortly afterwards, Bill retracted the flaps and she climbed more easily, gaining rapidly in speed and altitude.

Reaching our allotted height we began the long flight to the target. The fear evaporated as each member of the crew swung into the routine we'd practised for hours prior to this day, months of training paying off as the Lancaster joined the stream of others heading towards Occupied Europe. Around us 127 Lancasters and 4 Mosquitoes were travelling in the same direction but in the thickening cloud it seemed at first as if we were the only ones up aloft. When the clouds eventually thinned an amazing sight of hundreds of aircraft appeared, a metal armada all flying at the same altitude and direction in bright sunshine.

In what was only a short while, those who were able to caught their first sight of the French coastline and dark puffs filling the sky ahead warned them that the gunners below had been warned of our presence. Adrenaline coursed through our veins as these deadly smudges drew closer and light streams of multi-coloured flame, tracer, snaked up and whipped past at a bewildering speed. All around us heavy flak erupted in black smudges and flames, making the aircraft judder before rising and falling sharply in sudden, violent movements.

We skirted the deadly barrage and flew on, the only sound being navigator Ken Brown's voice giving quiet course corrections to Harry Brooker. Despite the time of year it was freezing at the altitude we had gained and not for the first time I was grateful for the warmth the aircraft heating provided. Aft of my operator's station the gunners cursed their heated suits as the thermostats roasted them one minute and froze them the next.

With the cold came tiredness, the tendency to droop one's eyelids for a second, however brief, and it was this threat that Harry Brooker strove to overcome. Periodically he would call up each of us to ensure our wakefulness as tired gunners could spell disaster for us all if a fighter attacked. Harry Brooker had an onboard system that relieved him of most of the strain of flying the Lancaster for hours on end. 'George' a rudimentary auto-pilot, gave him many hours of welcome relief during the long flights to and from the targets.

After three hours of flying, the target appeared 15,000ft below us amidst green fields surrounding the railway lines, wreathed in flak. In the clear evening air it seemed impossible to fly through the curtain of fire but Harry Brooker calmly flew straight and level after arming the bomb release switch whilst Bomb-aimer Dave Hector squinted through the bombsight as the railway yards came into sight below. Fragments of shells rattled against the metal skin of the airframe and the smell of cordite from near-misses filled our oxygen masks, leaving an acrid taste in one's mouth as we all willed him to press the bomb release.

'Bombs fused and selected.'

'Left-left. Steady. Right. Steady-steady... Bombs gone!' It took only moments and the Lancaster bucked upwards, freed from her load of fourteen 1,000lb bombs and Harry Brooker steadied the aircraft until he could bank the aircraft away from the billowing clouds of smoke below.

'Close bomb bay doors'.

'Affirmative. Bomb bay doors closed.'

'Looks like a direct hit, skipper!'

'Roger!' Harry replied quietly and then broke in as the chatter of excited men filled his ears. 'Keep quiet, you lot! Maintain radio silence and only use the RT if you see anything. Gunners, keep a close eye out for fighters.'

A chastened crew hastened to obey. Within my workspace, I was already sending a coded report, tapping on the Morse key and transmitting our position and ETA. We saw no enemy fighters nor the sight of the only Lancaster lost going down and after skirting the barrage of coastal flak on the return trip landed at Skellingthorpe, five hours and thirty-five minutes after we'd taken off.

A crew bus raced out and we boarded, all of us chattering frantically as we visibly relaxed. The sheer elation at surviving our first 'op' lent wings to the conversation and each of us tried to pour out our feelings of the experience at once. Eventually the rush of adrenaline faded and, dry-mouthed, most of us

reached for a welcome cigarette. After being quickly congratulated and de-briefed, we left the dispersal to trudge to the Mess for a meal. Bill Morgan caught us up.
'Heard the news, chaps?'
'What?'
'We did so well we're going back tomorrow!'
'You're kidding!'
'Straight up, they need us to go after some 'Buzz-bomb' sites.'
A collective groan rose up.
'Welcome to operations, chaps.'
No rest for the wicked, it seemed!'

That same day as they relaxed in the Mess, the Lancaster flown by Flt Lt William Reid VC, who had won his Victoria Cross as a pilot with 61 Sqn, was downed over France. Bill Reid's 617 Sqn aircraft ME557, S-Sugar, was hit by a 12,000lb Tallboy bomb dropped from a fellow squadron aircraft flying above him which broke the Lancaster in half. Only Bill Reid and his Wireless Operator F/O David Luker DFC, DFM survived, ending the war as POW's.

For Leslie, a typical 61 Squadron sequence on operations would be as follows: Once it was decided a night operation would take place that night the camp was sealed off from the outside world with no communication allowed, all the aircrew being barred from making outside telephone calls.

'One of the lads would poke his head round our room door and say, 'Operations tonight, chaps.'
I'd wave a hand by way of reply and walk up with the others to take part in an informal parade which determined how many aircrew were available for that

69

night. *Following that I'd walk over to the squadron office to peer at the notice board and see if my crew's name was on the battle-order sheet for the night's operation.*

By midday our aircraft would be checked over and any defects from the previous flight rectified by the ground crew. Any air tests required would now be carried out and the results discussed before deciding whether or not the aircraft was serviceable. If cleared to fly, it would then be refuelled and bombed-up in preparation for the night's take-off.

Without knowing at that time where the target was located, canny ground crew could work it out with a fair degree of certainty by checking the bomb load against the fuel. The Lancaster's full load was 2,154 gallons of high-octane fuel and it could carry approximately 14,000lbs of bombs. A large fuel requirement and small bomb-load would point to somewhere distant such as Berlin whereas minimum fuel and maximum bombs meant a target nearer Britain, such as France or Belgium.

Later that day, with fellow aircrew, I'd attend a Specialist Briefing for the Wireless Operators, Navigators and Bomb-aimers before joining the rest of the crew at the Main Briefing where the target would be announced and vital information discussed. At the Specialist Briefing we'd be given a copy of the Bomber Code for the day along with R/T (Voice.) and W/T (Morse.) call signs. Frequencies and call signs of stations were also issued plus colours for the time periods airborne. The codes were top secret and changed frequently, sometimes being issued on rice-paper so the wireless operator could eat them if the aircraft was shot down!

Next to come was supper, usually consisting of bacon and eggs and following that a walk to the

Locker Room to pick up my flying clothing, emergency rations, parachute and escape kit with the other crew members. Whilst there I'd test my flying helmet and oxygen mask on a special test rig before being taken out to the dispersal with our crew by bus to the aircraft. Squatting down on the grass next to our aircraft we'd sit around on a fine day, nervously smoking cigarette after cigarette or just talking until it was time to board. Dave Hector worked his nervous energy off by walking round the open bomb bay checking the bombs in their racks and ensuring that the safety release pins had all been removed. There was no point struggling over to the target to drop duds!

The signal would come and we'd clamber aboard the ladder placed against the rear hatch and wait for Harry Brooker to settle in and start the engines, ready to taxi to the runway for take-off. Whilst all that was happening I sat at my station in the aircraft and began to write up the operational log for the coming flight. Having one of the warmer seats in the aircraft by the hot air outlet meant I could fly in limited flying clothing whilst the gunners down the back froze in their bulky 'heated' suits.

61 Squadron shared Skellingthorpe with 50 Squadron and it had been agreed that 61 would approach the runway from the South and 50 Squadron from the North to avoid confusion and possible collisions. After the go-ahead had been given to proceed, a Lancaster from each squadron would take-off in turn with the Air Traffic Controller despatching as many as thirty Lancasters over a twenty-five minute period on a maximum-effort night.

Once airborne, I kept a listening watch for the first twenty minutes on the Skellingthorpe station transmitter frequency, Skellingthorpe's W/T call-sign being MR8. As the aircraft flew further from its base, I'd then switch over to 5 Group's frequency, call-sign 9SY and monitor it intently. Group transmissions were vital in sending out wind information for the Navigator to plot their course and also for sending recalls if the operation was cancelled.

Throughout the flight Group transmissions were sent at half-hour intervals preceded by a set of random numbers and on return the Wireless Operator's log would be closely scrutinised to ensure he'd logged all the relevant signals. Woe betide the unfortunate who had blank entries where he'd missed one or two!

On reaching the English coast the trailing aerial was reeled out behind the aircraft as all emergency calls, and SOS's were made on long wave. After crossing the enemy coast the aerial was reeled in again and in-between Group broadcasts I either stood with my head in the astrodome looking out for enemy fighters or resumed my seat to try and get a radio bearing to help the navigator fix his position. The view from the astrodome was spectacular and from its viewpoint I could see the hundreds of aircraft accompanying us until evening faded to night and they were lost in the darkness.

Before reaching the target I'd tune the VHF radio to the Master Bomber's frequency orbiting high overhead, allowing the Master Bomber to control the Main Force bombing efforts. Some nights he'd be in an affable mood but on other nights he'd be hectoring and badgering us over the radio, impatiently calling in the next wave and ordering re-marking of the target. All this with flak bouncing off the side of the aircraft and our aircraft shuddering and jerking around in the slipstream of the other aircraft in our vicinity. With so many of us in such a small area I always wondered *how we never had a mid-air collision but they did happen from time to time.*

It was an anxious time as we heard Dave Hector over the intercom giving Harry instructions to move the aircraft this way and that in order to enable him to release our bombs on the aiming point and no-one was more relieved than me when we felt the aircraft leap upwards as the bombs fell away. If we were carrying a 4,000lb blast bomb called a 'cookie' the aircraft seemed to climb even faster once it had been released but it was exhilarating to feel the upward rush. You never saw your own bombs go off, they were lost in the glare from thousands of bombs and incendiaries flashing upwards from the ground below. All I knew was that they were away and now we could get the hell out of there!

After we'd dropped our bombs and the requisite photograph taken, it was up to me to maintain a listening watch on the same VHF frequency waiting for the Master Bomber to order the Main Force home when he was satisfied with the results. During that anxious time over the target and beyond I also kept a watchful eye on the Fishpond screen, ready to shout out the order to corkscrew if I saw a fighter approaching fast.

The message to head for home having been received and relayed to the pilot, I could resume listening out for 5 Group transmissions as Harry Brooker turned our Lancaster away, noting weather conditions, cloud base and the barometric pressure prevalent at our home station. Half an hour away from landing I retuned the set to RAF Skellingthorpe's local frequency for local weather and landing instructions. Skellingthorpe's code was 'Black Swan' hence its nickname, 'Mucky Duck.' On approach we'd be given a number in the landing order unless we had wounded onboard or were badly damaged when we'd be brought straight in. Luckily, we never had occasion to need the emergency services

On landing, the aircraft taxied to the dispersal and shut down before the crew exited and we'd then make our way to a post-flight debriefing where a welcome mug of coffee with an added large measure of rum was consumed. On finishing being debriefed by the Intelligence Officers we'd stumble down the empty roads of the base to the accommodation and fall into bed. Sleep didn't always come easily, the adrenaline rush of the hours spent over enemy territory still kept us on a high, especially if you'd taken a Benzedrine tablet during the op to keep awake. For most of us it would be hours before you dropped off into a troubled sleep to contemplate one op less towards the magic figure required for survival.'

'Operation Overlord', the Allied invasion of Europe had taken place eight weeks earlier on 6th June when the Allies had stormed ashore on five beaches in Normandy. After a temporary stalemate, thousands of troops had pushed outwards from the beachheads, being supported by the RAF and Eight Air Force USAAF who took to daylight raids to bomb the enemy units below. Fierce fighting had ensued as the Germans were steadily pushed back and in retaliation for the landings, the Germans had launched the first of thousands of V1's ('*Vergeltungswaffe*'-Revenge weapon.) which were rocket-motor powered flying bombs at London on 13th June.

The V1, or 'Doodlebug' and 'Buzz-bomb' as it was nicknamed, was powered by a pulse-jet motor and launched from a 'ski-ramp' aimed in the compass direction of its target. Its range was worked out by simply adding or subtracting fuel for the engine. When the fuel was expended, the engine cut out and the bomb dropped onto its target. Over 9,500 in total were fired at Britain and the 2,200lb warheads caused 22,000 civilian casualties from the resulting explosions of their silent fall to earth.

It was decided that these sites liberally scattered around the Pas de Calais area of Northern France needed to be destroyed and an urgent order went out to Harris for his bombers to concentrate on this new menace. As the sites were small in area, night bombing was not an option so it was decided to adopt a campaign of daylight attacks. Understandably, many crews were perturbed at this proposition because as well as feeling vulnerable to flak and fighters during the day, they had to fly at much lower altitudes to ensure bombing accuracy.

Another decision which caused fury amongst the crews, soon rescinded, was that as the Air Ministry thought attacks on the V1 sites were easier than night attacks on Germany each V1 raid would only count as a third of an 'op' towards the magical number of thirty needed to complete a tour. In bald terms this meant that a crew flying only V1 raids would need to complete ninety such raids before their tour was considered to be expired.

The Brooker crew were unaware of this development as they droned steadily onto their target. A restless night's sleep had brought with it a hurried breakfast of bacon and eggs before the briefing for today's target, a V1 site at Mont Candon in the Pas de Calais. Poor weather meant that very few of the 385 Lancasters out of the 770 aircraft despatched bombed and they were not to know that this raid would set the pattern for the next few weeks.

'People often ask were we scared before an operation and the honest answer is, 'yes.' Being a relaxed sort of person I was more concerned with taking each day as it came, so any fear I felt was more a collective one for the crew and not purely for myself. Of course you heard of aircraft and aircrew that didn't

return and it did cross my mind that one day it might be us but you had to put those thoughts to the back of your mind and carry on. We fought a different kind of war as every operation meant we were in the front line, unlike a soldier or sailor who might see action only rarely Bomber Command crews faced the enemy at first hand each and every time they flew over enemy territory. I was just grateful that I flew with a good pilot and a crew whose approach to the whole business of operations meant that our chances of survival were that much better.

Every target was different but attacking those in the Ruhr, the industrialised heartland of Germany was more fraught. Not for nothing was the Ruhr called 'Happy Valley', the flak concentrations and nightfighter activity were amongst the heaviest in Europe and we always heaved a sigh of relief to find we weren't flying there. '

Ellon veteran Arthur Fry would agree with Leslie's sentiments. After completing his air gunner's training in early 1945, Arthur would squeeze his 5ft 11ins frame into the cramped rear turret of a 227 Sqn Lancaster of 5 Group operating out of Strubby, Lincolnshire. He vividly remembers the apprehension all of them suffered before take-off. Arthur summed up his experiences up follows: 'Although the heavy losses of 1943 had passed, there was always fear before take-off and elation on landing.'

Below are the raids the Brooker crew participated in with any relevant information present gleaned from 61 Squadron's Operations Log Book for those raids. The accompanying comments for those raids from Martin Middlebrook and Chris Everitt's superb reference book 'The Bomber Command Diaries' follow on in italics. All

MET: comments recorded in the commentary are weather conditions encountered over the target.

1. 31ˢᵗ July 1944. Joigny-Laroche.

QR-R. LL843. F/O. H.Brooker. Sgt. W.J.Morgan. F/O K.Brown. Sgt. D.J.Hector. **Sgt. L.B. Smith.** Sgt. W.P.Hunter. Sgt. A.D'Arcy. 'MET: Clear-good vis. Up 1732 down 2303. F/O Brooker bombed target visually with A.P in sights at 20.26hrs from 14,750ft. Bombing appeared concentrated and many fires were seen in target area. PHOTO: Ground detail.' 8 aircraft despatched, all returned safely.

127 Lancasters and 4 Mosquitoes of No's 1 and 5 Groups carried out an accurate raid on the railway yards at Joigny Laroche in clear conditions. 1 Lancaster lost.

2. 1ˢᵗ August 1944. Mont Candon.

QR-R. LL843. F/O H.Brooker. Sgt W.J.Morgan. F/O K.Brown. Sgt D.J.Hector. **Sgt L.B. Smith.** Sgt W.P.Hunter. Sgt A.D'Arcy. 'MET: 10/10ths cloud. Up 1655 down 2135. The mission was abandoned on instructions from the controller. F/O Brooker abandoned mission as instructed.' 13 aircraft despatched, all returned safely.

777 aircraft - 385 Lancasters, 324 Halifaxes, 67 Mosquitoes, 1 Lightning - to attack numerous V-weapon targets but only 79 aircraft were able to bomb; Bomber Command records do not state why the remaining sorties were abortive but poor weather conditions were the probable cause. No aircraft were lost.

3. 2nd August 1944. Bois de Cassan.

QR-R. LL843. F/O H.Brooker. Sgt W.J.Morgan. F/O K.Brown. Sgt D.J.Hector. **Sgt L.B.Smith.** Sgt W.P.Hunter. Sgt A.D'Arcy. 'MET: Clear. Up 1450 down 1910. F/O Brooker bombed from 16,000ft at 1718 hours. The aircraft formations were bad over the target but the raid appeared concentrated. Aircraft hit by flak.' 18 aircraft despatched, all returned safely.

394 aircraft - 234 Lancasters, 99 Halifaxes, 40 Mosquitoes, 20 Stirlings, 1 Lightning - attacked 1 flying bomb launch site and 3 supply sites. Visibility was clear at all targets and good bombing results were claimed. 2 Lancasters of No 5 Group lost from the raid on the Bois de Cassan supply site.

4. 3rd August 1944. Trossy St Maxim.

QR-R. LL843. F/O H.Brooker. Sgt W.J.Morgan. F/O K.Brown. Sgt D.J.Hector. **Sgt L.B. Smith.** Sgt W.P.Hunter. Sgt. A. D'Arcy. 'MET: Rather cloudy. Up 1150 down 1620. F/O Brooker observed no markers but considered the bombing too concentrated. Bombed from 18,000ft at 1432hrs.' 14 aircraft despatched, one failed to return.

1,114 aircraft - 601 Lancasters, 492 Halifaxes, 21 Mosquitoes - carried out major raids on the Bois de Cassan, Forêt de Nieppe and Trossy St Maxim flying-bomb stores. The weather was clear and all raids were successful. 6 Lancasters lost, 5 from the Trossy St Maxim raid and 1 from the Bois de Cassan raid. 1 Lightning and 1 RCM aircraft accompanied the raids.

One of the 5 Lancasters lost over Trossy St Maxim was a 61 Sqn aircraft, call-sign QR-L, registration PA162. F/O W.D Forbes was the only survivor, parachuting to safety behind the Allied lines. The following day, 4th August a posthumous VC was awarded to Sqn Leader I W

78

Bazalgette of 635 Sqn for his bravery when his Lancaster was shot down over Trossy St Maxim. The V1 site at Trossy St Maxim was heavily defended by scores of flak guns, making any operation against it fraught with danger, especially in daylight. Apart from the loss of QR-L, other 61 Sqn aircraft returned with varying degrees of flak damage.

5. 5th August 1944. St Leu d'Esserent.

QR-E. ND988. F/O H.Brooker. Sgt. W.J.Morgan. F/O K.Brown. Sgt D.J.Hector. **Sgt L.B.Smith.** Sgt W.P.Hunter. Sgt A. D'Arcy. 'MET: Cloudy. Up 1105 down 1535. F/O Brooker saw some smoke both from TI's and the target, concentrated bombing. Bombed from 15,000ft at 1335hrs.' 14 aircraft despatched, all returned safely.

742 aircraft - 469 Halifaxes, 257 Lancasters, 16 Mosquitoes - of No's 4, 5, 6 and 8 Groups attacked the Forêt de Nieppe and St Leu d'Esserent storage sites. Bombing conditions were good. 1 Halifax lost from the St Leu d'Esserent raid.

The flying bomb storage sites were housed in a number of caves with 25ft thick roofs dug into the limestone hillsides which had previously been used to grow mushrooms in before the war. Each 61 Sqn Lancaster's bomb load was 11,000lbs of mixed 1,000lb HE and 500lb bombs as the area was known to be heavily defended by flak batteries. Smoke and dust from the bombing reached 12,000ft, badly affecting accuracy.

6. 6th August 1944. Bois de Cassan.

QR-R. LL843. F/O H.Brooker. Sgt W.J.Morgan. F/O K.Brown. Sgt D.J. Hector. **Sgt L.B. Smith.** Sgt W.P.Hunter. Sgt A.D'Arcy. 'MET: Good vis. Up 0945 down 1430. F/O Brooker returned to base without bombing on instructions from the controller.' 9 aircraft despatched, all returned safely.

222 aircraft - 107 Lancasters, 105 Halifaxes, 10 Mosquitoes - of No's 4, 5 and 8 Groups attacked the Bois de Cassan and Forêt de Nieppe V-weapon sites. 1 Lightning accompanied the Bois de Cassan operation. The bombing at both targets was scattered. Some markers at Forêt de Nieppe were not accurate and some of the Master Bomber's instructions at Bois de Cassan were misunderstood, resulting in more than half of the bombing force there retaining their bombs. 3 Lancasters were lost on the Bois de Cassan raid.

7. 7/8th August 1944. Sequeville.
QR-W. ED470. F/O H.Brooker. Sgt W.J.Morgan. F/O K. Brown. Sgt D.J. Hector. **Sgt L.B.Smith.** F/Sgt N.M.Pettis (RCAF) Sgt A.D'Arcy. 'MET: Clear apart from ground haze. Up 2142 down 0150. F/O Brooker returned to base on instructions from controller. Dropped 7x1000USA at 4947N 0013E at 2354hrs.' 15 aircraft despatched, all returned safely.

1,019 aircraft - 614 Lancasters, 392 Halifaxes, 13 Mosquitoes - attacked five aiming points in front of Allied ground troops in Normandy. The attacks were carefully controlled - only 660 aircraft bombed and German strong points and the roads around them were well cratered. 10 aircraft - all Lancasters - were lost, 7 to German fighters, 2 to flak and 1 to an unknown cause.

8. 9/10th August 1944. Chatellerault.
QR-W. ED470. F/O H.Brooker. Sgt W.J.Morgan. F/O K. Brown. Sgt D.J.Hector. **Sgt L.B.Smith.** Sgt A.D'Arcy. W/O V.J.Burgess. 'MET: No cloud, very hazy. Up 2052 down 0311. F/O Brooker bombed from 5,300ft at 0015hrs. MPI

(Mean Point of Impact.) of 3 GTI. (Green Target Indicators.) Well concentrated attack.' 17 aircraft despatched, all returned safely.

176 Lancasters and 14 Mosquitoes of No 1 and 5 Groups successfully attacked an oil-storage dump at Forêt De Chatellerault. 2 Lancasters lost.

9. 11th August 1944. Bordeaux.

QR-P. **EE865.** F/O H.Brooker. Sgt W.J.Morgan. F/O K.Brown. Sgt D.J.Hector. **Sgt L.B. Smith**. Sgt. A.D'Arcy. W/O V.J.Burgess. 'MET: No cloud vis good. Up 1227 down 1505. *F/O Brooker returned early owing to oil leak in port outer engine.* 3x2000lb AP jettisoned safe 5350N 0130E at 1417hrs.' 9 aircraft despatched, all returned safely.

53 Lancasters and 3 Mosquitoes of No 5 Group attacked U-boat pens at Bordeaux and La Pallice with 2,000lb armour-piercing bombs, but examination of the pens after their capture a few weeks later showed that these bombs could not penetrate the roofs. 6 Mosquito fighters of No 100 Group provided a partial escort cover for the Bordeaux raid but no German fighters were encountered. No aircraft lost.

'The Bordeaux raid was the only one from which we returned early. The port outer lost all its oil and Harry Brooker shut the engine down to prevent it overheating. As stragglers, both outbound and inbound, were easy targets for the fighters he took the reluctant but correct decision to return to base. We jettisoned our bombs in the safe-designated area off the coast before landing back at Skellingthorpe.'

10.   12/13th August 1944. Rüsselsheim.

QR-W   ED470.   F/O H.Brooker. Sgt W.J.Morgan. F/O K.Brown. Sgt. D.J.Hector. **Sgt L.B. Smith**. Sgt A.D'Arcy. W/O V.J.Burgess. 'MET: Hazy-visibility good. Up 2146 down 0255. F/O Brooker bombed MPI of red and green TI's. Reported good concentration of fires in target area. Fires seen for 60/70 miles after leaving target. Suspected considerable fighter activity. PHOTO: Target condition failure-fires and haze.' 15 aircraft despatched, one failed to return.

297 aircraft - 191 Lancasters, 96 Halifaxes, 10 Mosquitoes - to Rüsselsheim. 13 Lancasters and 7 Halifaxes lost, 6.7 per cent of the force. The target for this raid was the Opel motor factory and normal Pathfinder marking methods were used. The motor factory was only slightly damaged; the local report states that the tyre and dispatch departments and the powerhouse were hit but most of the bombs fell in open countryside south of the target.

Call-sign QR-H, registration ME596 from 61 Sqn was one of the 13 Lancasters lost. F/O J.Meek was the only survivor. Lost with the aircraft was F/S C.Scrimshaw, at 39 one of the oldest Bomber Command aircrew to be lost in the war. Also lost was F/S K. Burnside DFM, on his second tour of operations.

'Rüsselsheim was our crew's third night raid after Bomber Command was released from army support duties following D-Day and resumed its night bombing campaign against German targets. It always felt strange taking off in the late evening and navigating to the target through darkened, hostile skies. Searchlights moving around the skies in a seemingly aimless pattern were to be feared as was

the flak and nightfighters were out in force that night, claiming many victims.

We were briefed to dive and corkscrew away if 'coned' by the searchlights. Once you were lit up by one the rest would quickly swing round and pin you in the glare, blinding the pilot and hoping to drive you down to a lower altitude where the light flak would soon rip the aircraft to shreds. We were lucky that night but were to see many of our aircraft fall victim in this manner in the months to come.

Ignoring the blinding flashes all around us, QR-W bombed on the Target Indicators as instructed and we swung gratefully for home, landing in the cold dawn to a hot meal before sinking gratefully into our beds. There was very little chit-chat amongst us on landing, I remember, just an overwhelming sense of weariness.'

11. 25/26th August 1944. Darmstadt.

QR-T.   NF914.   F/O H.Brooker. Sgt W.J.Morgan. F/O K.Brown. Sgt D.J.Hector. **Sgt. L.B.Smith**. F/Sgt S.Calver. W/O V.J. Burgess. 'MET: No cloud-some haze. Up 2035 down 0450. F/O Brooker bombed centre of cluster of red TI's at 0123hrs from 8,500ft. Much smoke and many incendiary fires were seen. Bombing was concentrated although the markers seemed rather scattered. PHOTO: Ground detail.' 18 aircraft despatched, one failed to return.

190 Lancasters and 6 Mosquitoes of No 5 Group to Darmstadt which had not been seriously attacked by Bomber Command before. 7 Lancasters lost. This 'No 5 Group method' raid was a failure. The Master Bomber had to return early; his 2 deputies were shot down; the flares were dropped too far west and the low-level Mosquito marker aircraft could not locate the target.

95 buildings were hit and 8 people were killed by the scattered bombs which did hit Darmstadt. 33 of the Lancasters bombed other targets, including at least 13 aircraft which joined in the successful raid on nearby Rüsselsheim.

Call-sign QR-O, registration PA162 from 61 Sqn was one of the 7 Lancasters lost, the aircraft crashing near the town of Gross-Gerau. Three aircrew survived, F/O S.Fleming RCAF, WO1. E.Lewis RCAF and Sgt P.Dunkley.

Lancaster QR-T was a new aircraft, only two weeks old, a replacement for the aircraft lost on the Stuttgart raid of 28/29th July. It's first flight was the Rüsselsheim raid of 12th August and it would be lost to flak over Calais on 24th September.

12. 26/27th August 1944. Königsberg.

QR-T. NF914. F/O H.Brooker. Sgt W.J.Morgan. F/O K.Brown. Sgt D.J.Hector. **Sgt L.B.Smith**. W/O V.J.Burgess. Sgt W.P.Hunter. 'MET: No cloud-good vis. Up 2022 down 0627. F/O Brooker bombed centre of red TI's at 0118hrs from 9,000ft. Reported attack to be well concentrated. Two fires seen just short of target. PHOTO: Ground detail.' QR-T Diverted to Milltown on return.17 aircraft despatched, all returned safely.

174 Lancasters of No 5 Group to Königsberg, which was an important supply port for the German Eastern Front. The route to the target was 950 miles from the No 5 Group bases. Photographic reconnaissance showed that the bombing fell in the eastern part of the town but no report is available from the target, now Kaliningrad in Lithuania. 4 Lancasters lost.

13. August 29/30th 1944. Königsberg.

QR-T.   NF914. F/O H.Brooker. Sgt W.J.Morgan. F/O K.Brown.   F/Sgt   D.J.Hector.   **Sgt   L.B.Smith.**   Sgt W.P.Hunter. Sgt A.D'Arcy. 'MET: Cloud base 9,000ft. Good visibility.   Up 2038 down 2300.   F/O Brooker identified target visually aided by flares but did not bomb. Received orders from controller 'Do not bomb.' After completing two orbits of the target and two bombing runs did not bomb as Controller ordered him to wait. Decided to abandon mission owing to fuel shortage and to fact that VHF Receiver weak and distorted over target area. Great congestion caused by orbiting and weather conditions.' (Landed at Ludford Magna on return. Short of fuel.) 16 aircraft despatched, one failed to return.

189 Lancasters of No 5 Group carried out one of the most successful No 5 Group attacks of the war on Königsberg at extreme range. Only 480 tons of bombs could be carried because of the range of the target but severe damage was caused around the 4 separate aiming points selected. This success was achieved despite a 20 minute delay in opening the attack because of the presence of low cloud; the bombing force waited patiently, using up precious fuel, until the marker aircraft found a break in the clouds and the Master Bomber, Wing Commander J Woodroffe, probably No 5 Group's most skilled Master Bomber, allowed the attack to commence. Bomber Command estimated that 41 per cent of all the housing and 20 per cent of all the industry in Königsberg were destroyed. There was heavy fighter opposition over the target and 15 Lancasters, 7.9 per cent of the force, were lost.

As they left the target they would have seen the glare of the burning town following them all the way to the Baltic.

The centre of the historic town was ripped out by the bombs and incendiaries that rained down on it. The original quarters of Altstadt, Löbenicht and Kneiphof were completely destroyed, along with the cathedral, the castle, and all the churches of the old city, the university and the shipping quarters.

Among the aircraft taking part in the Königsberg raid were two Lancasters which had both flown over 100 operations. ED588, VN-G on its 128th operation crashed in Sweden, one of four 50 Squadron aircraft lost that night. ED860, VR-N *Nan*, of 61 Squadron returned safely to Skellingthorpe from her 129th operation with severe damage from a nightfighter's 20mm cannon shell to her wing root and starboard inner fuel tank.

After undergoing lengthy repairs and completing only one further 'op' in October, on the night of 28th October 1944, VR-N, *Nan*, crashed whilst taking-off on a raid to Bergen which would have been her 131st operation. She hit a Glim light on the runway and burst a tyre, causing the undercarriage to collapse and the stricken Lancaster slid for some distance with a full bomb load, pouring fuel from a ruptured tank before coming to rest. The crew hurriedly exited the wreckage but *Nan* retained her reputation as a lucky aircraft by not exploding and she was stripped down and struck off charge, an ignominious end to such a fine aircraft.

The Squadron CO was so enraged at what he thought was an avoidable accident that he made the unfortunate pilot, an Australian Pilot Officer called Pearce, go round all the ground trade huts and apologise to the ground 'erks' for his actions.

Leslie's recollections of the first Königsberg raid on 26th August were far from favourable:

'After a long, cold flight over the Baltic and having successfully dropped our bombs on the target, on the return trip I picked up an urgent CQ-CQ-CQ message ordering us to divert to Milltown in Northern Scotland. Milltown was RAF Lossiemouth's satellite station and we were being sent there as fog was blanketing Lincolnshire. An indifferent welcome awaited us, cold, damp Nissen huts and instead of a well-earned breakfast of bacon and eggs the station chefs threw together a poor meal which did nothing to lift our already low spirits.

No conquering heroes welcome, it seemed to us that by landing at Milltown we were a nuisance to the camp who had to feed, accommodate and refuel us. They couldn't get rid of us quickly enough but our departure was delayed for various reasons until ten the following morning. Eventually we took off and landed at one pm at Skellingthorpe only to be given the grim news that we'd be returning to Königsberg that evening at six thirty. The Main Force marker aircraft had crashed eleven miles short of the target and the following illuminator flares were dropped according to plan but in the wrong place.

A thoroughly disgruntled crew just had time to bolt down a quick meal and attend the various briefings before the squadron aircraft were fuelled, bombed-up, guns loaded and packets of 'Window' stored in the fuselage. Soon after that we picked up our flight bags and flying clothing and trudged wearily back to a different aircraft, as our own Lancaster QR-T had become unserviceable at the last moment.

Forming up over Flamborough Head we began climbing out over the North Sea for the Baltic with Ken Jones and myself furiously computing courses and logging events. An alert enemy had gathered scores of nightfighters and we witnessed scores of air *combats all the way over the Baltic and target area. One of my tasks was to log the times we saw aircraft going down, a grim reminder of the task in hand. Luckily, no fighters came near us but near-misses from the flak caused us some anxious moments before we cleared the target. A delay in dropping our bombs due to the Master Bomber waiting for more favourable bombing conditions used up precious fuel and we were forced to land at Ludford Magna on our return after a gruelling eleven hours in the air.'*

14. 31st August 1944. Rollencourt.

QR-Y. ME595. F/L H.Brooker. Sgt W.J.Morgan. F/O K.Brown. F/S D.J.Hector. **Sgt L.B. Smith.** Sgt W.P.Hunter. Sgt A.D'Arcy. 'MET: Good visibility. Up 1615 down 1950. F/L Brooker bombed from 14,000ft at 1817hrs with good visibility. Observed smoke up to 4,000ft from a wood which was on fire. One white smoke puff seen south of target. Concentrated bombing.' 15 aircraft despatched, all returned safely.

601 aircraft - 418 Lancasters, 147 Halifaxes, 36 Mosquitoes - to attack 9 sites in Northern France where the Germans were believed to be storing V-2 rockets. 8 of the sites were found and bombed. 6 Lancasters lost.

It's quite amazing reading through the Operations Log of the months of July and August 1944 to realise how many aircraft returned from an operation with their bombs still onboard. Some entries give locations where bombs were dropped in the sea before landing at Skellingthorpe but many more entries tell of aircraft after aircraft returning with their bomb loads intact. The effort in sending these aircraft over Europe with seven men onboard, against enemy flak and fighters, only for them to return without having dropped any bombs at all seems such a waste, akin to sending soldiers into battle and instructing them not to fire their weapons!

Rollencourt was to be their last operation with 61 Squadron. They had carried out 14 operations, four at night and the rest daylight raids. Four of these daylight raids were flown on consecutive days, between the 31st July and 3rd August. Their fourteen raids were carried out in a month, during which time they would brief, take-off and fly to the target, bomb, fly back and land, exhausted. On every one of those raids they were fired at by an enemy who was doing his best to kill them, something to concentrate the minds of even the most easy-going of men.

'Everyone was conscious of the empty beds signifying those crews who didn't return and the lack of a familiar face in the Mess told its own story. It was common to leave your locker keys behind before a raid so as to make it easier to empty the locker should you fail to return. Many left last letters on their beds before flying, with instructions as to how and what to do with their belongings 'in the event of...' I know, I did exactly that on every raid.

Some crews had lucky mascots draped around the cockpit or performed rituals such as peeing on the tailwheel before boarding. We had none that I remember and relied on each other to see us through.'

In the air it was the vigilant crews who survived, in the main. Flak was a matter of pure luck but the fighters were a different story. Tired crews got 'the chop', along with the careless and the overconfident. A crew that worked together as a team and were vigilant all the way out and back stood a better chance of survival than those who relaxed their lookout. Once clear of the target area some aircraft captains were known to allow their gunners to leave their turrets on the return leg and enjoy a smoke. Such recklessness did not last long.

Harry Brooker would have none of it. After leaving the target, Leslie would stand for many hours looking out through the perspex bubble of the astrodome to take star shots for the navigator and keeping a careful watch for fighters. From his lofty perch he witnessed many beautiful sunsets after an evening take-off and tracer streams in the darkness of the night that told of airborne combats, together with multi-coloured splashes below as the bombs landed.

'The relentless strain of operations took its toll. People weighed up their chances of surviving a tour and became all too aware of the odds stacked against them. Being half-way through a tour didn't guarantee survival, one could get the chop on one's twentieth 'op', as well as one's first, in the end it all came down to luck.

During our time at Skellingthorpe we became automatons like so many aircrew that ate, slept, flew, packed in the 'shoot pontoon' craze they'd previously enjoyed, drank far too much beer for relaxation and chased girls whenever the opportunity presented itself. With very little success, it must be said, on my part in the latter!'

Girls were still a mystery to a lot of the young men who flew nightly raids against the country's enemies. Although the war had brought a loosening of morals, sex for many was only to be enjoyed as a part of marriage. Leslie's parent's advice on loose women helped preserve his virginity and any association he had at various dance halls and pubs with the fairer sex at this time was on a purely platonic basis. It didn't help that one or two of his crew loved chasing women and regaled him with lurid tales of passion-filled encounters but after one of them suffered a beating from a jealous husband harmony was restored to the crew and the tales of sex and debauchery stopped. It might seem strange in this enlightened age to think that sex was not openly discussed or read about but for many people it was a taboo subject with even the most casual depiction of female nudity being frowned upon. Young men with all the natural curiosity and urges of their age were expected to forego any informal relationships and concentrate on the task of winning the war.

Even more hidden from sight and never discussed was the subject of homosexuality. In these enlightened days being 'gay' as it now known, bears little stigma but in the sexually-repressed 1940's to admit to being a homosexual was to become a loathed and derided figure and in the services a position that would meet with severe consequences.

Leslie's boyish good looks attracted many members of the opposite sex so it was with some confusion and fear that he encountered an approach from a member of his own sex. After an evening's drinking, the Station Warrant Office, the SWO, a feared figure in RAF Station life, accompanied Leslie back to the accommodation block where he, too, lived and casually asked Leslie back to his room for a last drink. He cited a mutual interest in 'The Search for Truth' but once in the room made clumsy advances and after administering a sharp elbow, Leslie fled to the safety of his own barracks.

It was a different relationship that developed when flying together. In the air they had quickly settled down to a strict regime of discipline and co-operation with each other. The sight of a burning city below them or their bombs exploding on a clear day far below had long since lost its fascination. What was left in its place was a grim determination to complete the task and survive. They had seen the results of flak or enemy fighters tearing a large bomber apart in a fiery ball and had no wish to emulate those poor unfortunates falling out of the sky in front of their shocked and apprehensive eyes.

Leslie's tasks multiplied as he furiously logged Bomber Command's airborne amendments to briefing topics and passed them on to Harry Brooker or Ken Brown. Requests to transmit so a radio station could fix their position with a 'QDM' (Query Direction Magnetic.) were practised by him again and again. A badly-shot up aircraft approaching England would transmit an emergency 'Darky' call and the receiving station would then give them a magnetic bearing (QDM.) to fly. Many such aircraft made it back safely to base only because of this feature and a good WOP/AG was worth his weight in gold to his crew if he was on the ball.

A significant piece of news awaited them on returning to Skellingthorpe from Rollencourt. Their transformation from a 'green' crew into one who quietly got on with the war with good results had not gone unnoticed. Harry Brooker called them together to inform them that their names were on Standing Orders as having been selected to join the Pathfinder Force. After a brief deliberation they agreed to go with him rather than break the crew up and have to start over again with strangers. It would mean stretching their tour, though, from thirty to forty five and they were already nearly half-way through a normal tour.

Finishing the normal tour would mean a welcome respite from the strain of operations but to a man they decided their future lay in the safe hands of Harry Brooker. After all, as Leslie explained, better the devil you knew than the devil you didn't. Two days later, an experienced crew with those fourteen operations under their belt, they left 61 Squadron and Skellingthorpe to join 97 (Straits Settlement) Squadron at its home base just down the road at RAF Coningsby.

'It wasn't too much of a decision to be made, we followed Harry Brooker to 97 squadron because we had faith in his abilities as a pilot and faith in the Lancaster to bring us home from each operation under Harry's guiding hands. We had a good pilot and a great aircraft and feeling that we'd blended well together it gave us confidence in overcoming any disaster in the times yet to come.'

Sharing Coningsby with them was their sister Pathfinder squadron, No.83, giving the airbase a total of over forty Lancasters housed there. Each squadron had approximately twenty-four Lancasters on charge, in three flights of eight aircraft. They would arrive with mixed feelings though, pride at being selected but also apprehension of what lay ahead.

Leslie Bruce Smith Pictured in 2011

The tail and wreckage of a German Heinkel He-111, shortly after crashing into the uncompleted ice-rink in South Aberdeen, 12th July 1940. Spitfires from 603 Sqdn shot the bomber down in flames.

**Images of the Aberdeen Blitz, 21st April 1943 and how the properties now look when revisited in 2010.
Top: Hilton Avenue. Middle: Elmbank Road. Bottom: King's Cross Terrace.**

Photographs courtesy of Grampian Police Archives.

Leslie (underneath dotted line.) and fellow wireless operators..
Compton Bassett 1942.

Leslie seated, front row second left, in 1943 on his WOP/AG's course.

TOP. WOP/AG Leslie Smith, extreme right, top row at No.9 Advanced Flying Training Unit, Llandwrog, North Wales, 1943.
BOTTOM. Christmas Day menu, Llandwrog, 1943.

The deadly side of the air war. Summer, 1944, a 97 Squadron Lancaster stands at its dispersal being loaded with 1000lb General Purpose bombs.

Getting ready to go. The seven strained faces of a 97 Squadron crew about to board their Avro Lancaster, 1944.

Photographs courtesy of Kevin Bending.

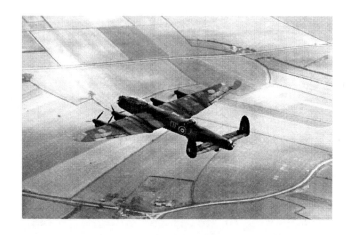

A 97 Squadron Lancaster OF-J returning home from a raid over Europe. Note the two feathered engines on the port wing.

Photographs courtesy of Kevin Bending.

Group Captain Peter Johnson DSO OBE DFC AFC Commanding Officer 97 Squadron 1944-45, standing with his crew and members of his ground crew in front of Lancaster OF-D, March 1945.

'B' Flight, 97 Squadron at Coningsby, 1945. Leslie is believed to be in there…somewhere.

Photographs courtesy of Kevin Bending.

HEADQUARTERS,

PATH FINDER FORCE,

ROYAL AIR FORCE.

14th December, 1944.

To : 1345377 Sergeant Smith, L.B.

AWARD OF PATH FINDER FORCE BADGE

You have to-day qualified for the award of the
Path Finder Force Badge and re entitled to wear the
Badge as long as you remain in the Path Finder Force.

2. You will not be entitled to wear the Badge
after you leave the Path Finder Force without a further
written certificate from me authorising you to do so.

Air Vice-Marshal, Commanding
Path Finder Force.

(1000) M23608/3093 12/44 2m BGH Gp573.

**The rather crumpled document awarding Sgt Leslie
Smith the Pathfinder Force badge. It is signed by Air
Vice-Marshall Don Bennett, the Founding Father of the
Pathfinders.**

Warrant Officer Leslie Bruce Smith pictured here in April 1945 standing beside a Lancaster wheel-well at RAF Coningsby.

Dear Leslie,

All year I have intended to drop you a line but like many good intentions it has not been fulfilled.

Believe me I was lucky to have such a good crew in 1944/45. It was that and Lady Luck ~~that was~~ why we survived and you carried out your part with calm efficiency - and a good job too!

How did you come to lose your Log Book? Since you were with me on all 38 trips perhaps I could copy the details from my Log Book and then your Grandson would have to believe the two trips to Koningsberg, Politz (Stettin) etc! You may recall I was trained in Canada. Next June, after 50 years, Margo & I are going to a Wartime Pilots etc Reunion in Winnipeg and we will be over there for 3 weeks in total, spending a week in Ontario and a week in the Rockies.

Hope you, Bess & the family are well,

Harry.

One of the first letters Leslie received from his former skipper, Harry Brooker, after a gap of twenty years. In it, Harry verifies the 38 operations they carried out together as a crew.

Bomber's certificate is found

KE 7/12/01

A HISTORIC certificate dedicated to a war hero has turned up in the North-east.

The document was handed to Inverurie's new branch of the Royal Air Forces Association.

It was awarded to a Flight Sergeant Smith and personally signed by Air Vice-Marshal Donald Bennett, legendary leader of the Path Finder Force.

The World War 2 pathfinders – members of RAF Bomber Command – were renowned for their skill, courage, and determination.

The certificate was given to Inverurie's Royal British Legion for the RAFA archive, without any clue to its history.

Branch historian, Newmachar-based picture framer Bruce Sutherland has made a copy of the certificate.

He said he would be happy to hand the framed original over to the airman's relatives.

Anyone who may be related to Sgt Smith can get further information from Mr Sutherland on 01651 862215.

"Green Hell" Exploit Preferred To Shop Work

Jungle Adventure For Aberdeen Butcher

A TWENTY-FOUR-YEAR-OLD butcher will hang up his apron and quit his counter in Aberdeen soon to seek adventure in the Amazonian jungle.

He is Mr Leslie B. Smith, 637 Holburn Street, the second Aberdeen man to be accepted for an expedition to explore the "green hell" of the Amazon valley.

The expedition will set out within the next few weeks.

It is being led by Captain Claud R. Spriggs, a forty-six-year-old Leicester mariner. As already announced, one of its members will be Mr Graeme Robertson, 29 Thomson Street, Aberdeen.

Mr Smith and Mr Robertson are close friends.

They were in the Boys' Brigade together and joined the R.A.F. together. There they parted, Mr Robertson joining the Air Sea Rescue Service, while Mr Smith went to Bomber Command as a wireless-operator air gunner.

It is in the capacity of a wireless

Mr Leslie B. Smith served with

Two clippings that appeared in the local press over the years, describing the finding of Leslie's Pathfinder Certificate and a description from 1946 of his proposed trip to the Amazon Basin in search of Colonel Fawcett.

Chapter Four

It soon became apparent that allowing bombers to navigate their own way to the target and bomb on their own cognisance was an unreliable way of obtaining the best results. The mounting losses incurred following such a creed were a cause for grave concern within the Air Ministry and it was decided to form specialist units who would light up, or 'mark', targets for the aircraft of the Main Force who would follow. In this way the bombs dropped would land in a tighter pattern and cause maximum damage.

The Germans had already demonstrated that this type of target identification could be achieved by the use of *Kampfgeschwader 100* and its Heinkel He111 aircraft, when they used bombing aids such as *'Knickebein'* (Crooked Leg.) to devastate Coventry as early as the 14th November 1940. It was only natural that the British would develop their own aids and the formation of a specialist marking force was the natural progression of this, even if it did meet with vehement opposition at its inception.

Accordingly, in 1942, Air Chief Marshall Harris was ordered to strip his Groups of their more experienced crews to form the backbone of this new unit, which would be known as the 'Pathfinder Force.' Unsurprisingly, Harris was most reluctant to follow this course, preferring to have each Group form its own specialist target-marking squadrons but he was overruled. Ignoring the pleas from the Groups that stripping out their best crews would deprive them of much-needed expertise, the Pathfinder Force, or PFF, came into being in July 1942. It was given the designation of No. 8 Group, Pathfinder Force and the motto, 'We Guide to Strike.'

To give Harris his due, once he'd been overruled he set to with a vengeance to ensure the PFF got off to a perfect start. Its leader was to be an Australian and already acclaimed pilot and navigator, Donald Bennett. At only 31, very young to be a Group Captain, his flying abilities and operational experience was described by Harris as, *"altogether exceptional."* A brilliant navigator with extensive pre-war long-distance flight-proving experience, Promoted to the rank of Air Commodore, Bennett had previously qualified as a pilot and flew operations at the start of the war, commanding both No.10 and 77 Squadrons. Shot down over Trondheim in 1942, he evaded capture and escaped back to England via Sweden.

Not one to suffer fools lightly, Bennett demanded and obtained the very best for his crews. Four squadrons were initially taken from their respective Groups and housed adjacent to each others airfields. They were: No's 7 (Stirlings.), 35 (Halifaxes.), 83 (Lancasters.) and No156 (Wellingtons.). In April 1943, two new squadrons arrived, 405 (Halifaxes.) and 97 (Lancasters.) Eventually, the other aircraft types were phased out and the PFF employed the Lancaster and twin-engined Mosquito for the rest of the war.

Their debut into the art of target-marking came on the night of 18/19th August 1942, when 31 aircraft from 7, 35, 83 and 156 squadrons marked the town of Flensburg in Northern Germany. The attempt was a dismal failure but that failed to deter Bennett who pressed on with attracting the best crews into his new command.

The early crews were the cream of Bomber Command; many had flown multiple operations and some were on second tours, with chests bearing the medal ribbons of recognition to their gallantry. A 'tour' on Main Force bomber operations was completed after thirty operations when the lucky survivors would be stood down from operations for a minimum of six months. Aircrew joining a Pathfinder squadron agreed to fly at least forty-five operations without a break although most would go on to serve many more. Logbooks containing sixty, seventy, even eighty op were not uncommon. One of the most courageous Master Bomber's of all, Group Captain Leonard Cheshire VC, was taken off operations having completed 103 operations.

In later times crews were welcomed into the PFF who, whilst not having a great deal of experience, showed great promise. Later still, crews who had passed out top of their training were accepted before they'd even flown their first operation. A keen eye was kept for those showing the right qualities and any attempt by Station Commanders at dumping 'problem' crews on the PFF resulted in them being swiftly weeded out.

To distinguish them from the rest of Bomber Command, PFF crews were awarded a brass RAF Eagle badge which was proudly worn on the left breast below the uniform pocket. The badge was awarded as a temporary measure after a number of 'proving' operations had been carried out (Eight in Leslie's case.) and could then be worn permanently at the end of ones tour. Along with the badge came a certificate signed by Don Bennett himself and Leslie's has miraculously survived, to be included in this story.

The new airborne technology then entering service, GEE, and in particular, *H2S* and OBOE, was enthusiastically embraced and fitted to Pathfinder aircraft. New methods of marking targets were developed, with different colour combinations of TI's (Target Indicators.) employed to ensure maximum results.

OBOE was a sophisticated airborne radar device capable of impressive results in thick cloud and was almost exclusively used by the PFF alone. Flying on an arc to within ten minutes of the target the aircraft would pick up the first OBOE pulse, nicknamed 'CAT' and relay it back to the transmitting station in England. Knowing the aircraft's prearranged height and speed, the CAT measured the aircraft's distance from it and issued a set of dots and dashes, informing the pilot if he was veering to one side or the other of the arc. A continuous note, OBOE, told him he was on course. A second transmitting station, known as the 'MOUSE', plotted the bomber's course along the arc and as the aircraft reached the correct point the MOUSE would cut in with a sharp tone, at which point the bomb-aimer released his bombs or marker TI's. OBOE was used exclusively by Pathfinder Mosquitoes, with GEE and H2S being carried by the Lancaster.

With H2S giving a plan view of the ground below and OBOE giving precise release information, the ability to accurately mark a target hundreds of miles away in all weathers for the following waves to saturate with bombs became a reality. Because of the complexity of these navigational aids, most Pathfinder aircraft flew with eight crewmen, the normal complement plus an extra navigator. The usual navigator carried on with his normal duties and the other operated the H2S set.

Broadly speaking, the PFF crews would man up and navigate their way to the designated target ahead of the Main Force. Once over the target, TI's would be dropped on the aiming point and the Main Force would then arrive and bomb on the coloured markers. A new concept, that of 'Master Bomber', or 'Master of Ceremonies', with a Deputy Master Bomber also came into being. The Master Bomber and his crew would orbit the target and direct the bombing, using 'Supporters' to ensure the bomber stream arrived over the correct target area and bringing in 'Backer-ups' to remark the target when necessary.

Three types of marking were used, PARAMATTA, NEWHAVEN, and WANGANUI, being chosen by Bennett to reflect place-names from the Antipodes. PARAMATTA was a straight–forward method of marking the target using Target Indicators for the Main Force to aim at. The 'Backer-ups' would then remark the target area or MPI

(Mean Point of Impact.) as bombs obscured or smothered the TI's. NEWHAVEN utilised dropping flares to precisely illuminate the target and other PFF aircraft would then drop their coloured TI's and the last method, WANGANUI, involved dropping TI's on parachutes when the target was obscured by smoke or thick cloud but had been identified by OBOE-equipped aircraft.

This, then, was the force Harry Brooker and his crew joined in the early days of September 1944. Having fourteen operations already under their belt they were not newcomers to the field but a crew who knew the score and had seen at first hand the deadly game being played out nightly in the skies over Europe. In time they would be proud to wear the brass hovering eagle emblem of the Pathfinder Force under their aircrew brevet after the required proving flights and join in with their colleagues in taking to the skies ahead of the Main Force. 3,700 Pathfinder Force members were killed on operations, a small but significant number of the total number of aircrew deaths in the war.

By giving up their Manchesters in 1942, 97 Squadron (Straits Settlement.) became the second RAF squadron to be equipped with the Lancaster, following 44 Squadron, who were the first. Although 8 Group were the designated Pathfinder group, 5 Group commanded by The Right Honourable Sir Ralph Cochrane had two Lancaster PFF squadrons attached, No's 83 and 97. A further PFF Mosquito squadron, 627, also served with 5 Group whose Headquarters in 1944 were at Morton Hall, Swinderby.

The Group structure was further sub-divided into Bases and 97 Squadron formed part of 54 Base. Established in 1943, 54 Base comprised of the squadrons based at RAF Coningsby, RAF Skellingthorpe and RAF Metheringham, all located in Lincolnshire.

The rank structure on a Pathfinder base differed slightly from that of a bomber base, being as follows:
Station Commander was an Air Commodore.
Squadron Commander was a Group Captain.
Flight Commander was a Wing Commander.
Deputy Flight Commander was a Squadron Leader.

'Based at RAF Coningsby alongside 83 Sqn when Harry Brooker and our crew arrived to join them on August 2nd 1944, 97 Squadron's motto was 'Achieve Your Aim.' After the privations of Skellingthorpe, Coningsby was a delight. It contained permanent blocks with hygienic amenities and possessed a comfortable Sergeants and Warrant Officers Mess. From our very first day we were made aware of our elite status and the attentions of the mess servants filled us with a confidence that here was a worthwhile job to be done.

The Flight Commander, Wing Commander Baker, harangued us during a fierce opening lecture in which he drove home his demands on our fledgling crew, warning us to be ready in a few hours time for a 'proving flight.' Baker proved to be a hard taskmaster, demanding the utmost from his crews and woe betide anyone whose standards slipped. He drove them all hard in his efforts to gain the maximum effort from them and whilst resented by many, others could see the need for discipline. Our lives would depend on each others adherence to the procedures and rules of the air.'

Our first aircraft was a different matter. OF-Q was an overhauled aircraft from the maintenance pool, replacing one lost in action with its crew. OF-E and OF-K were Lancasters the Brooker crew flew in for most of their operations but for the time being, as a new crew we flew a variety of different Lancs. Getting

113

straight into our new routine, familiarisation flights around the surrounding countryside, circuits and bumps and fighter affiliation exercises became the norm, all of which involved heavy work for my wireless operator skills.

Coningsby also had a swimming pool and it was in that environment we practised dinghy drills, a vital exercise in providing us with as realistic an experience in preparation for the day, when, God forbid, we might find ourselves abandoning an aircraft in the water for real.

A week after joining Coningsby, on the 9th September, I was pleased to find out that I'd been promoted to Flight Sergeant with the other sergeants in the crew and that Harry Brooker was now a Flight Leuitenant. Moving to the PFF automatically meant a step up of one rank and the increased pay and privileges were a welcome addition.

It was at Coningsby that I threw myself enthusiastically into camp life, finding a talent to entertain in the Sgts/WO's Mess. Over the coming months, organising Race Night's, Dances, Beanos and Talent Nights became a regular feature of camp life. My talent for pontoon never quite took off but what I lost on the cards I gained in a certain prowess on the snooker table. On some occasions I could be persuaded to stand up and sing, a talent that brought adoring WAAF's into my social life, a very welcome distraction from the strain of operations.

Outside the base, The White Swan in Coningsby had the attraction of a charming barmaid, a half-decent pint and an off-tune piano that I could be persuaded to play on occasion. The small nearby fishing port of Boston held more places for relaxation and I was lucky enough to be able to indulge a passion for roller-skating, the exercise giving me a chance to *work off the nervous energy and tension that operations brought to us all.*

It was also a chance to meet young women not involved in the services but aware that as our crew's number of operations increased our chances of survival decreased, I tended to keep female company at arm's length. Having seen the grief that close relationships brought when a crew failed to return I felt it better not to get too close, becoming quite insular like a lot of aircrew in this outlook.'

Every new crew had at least two weeks intensive Pathfinder training before being passed competent for operations and it was during this time that Leslie was handed another duty to add to those he already carried out in the air. He was informed that he would be the aircraft's FISHPOND operator, a new radar warning system for detecting enemy fighters.

When Butch Harris was made aware of the Luftwaffe using the transmissions from the rear-warning radar *Monica* to home in on the bombers he immediately ordered the system to be removed from all RAF aircraft. In its place came FISHPOND, an offshoot from the *H2S* ground-mapping radar already carried by Pathfinder aircraft. A feed from the *H2S* was fed to a display mounted at the wireless operator's left shoulder and from his seat he was able to monitor the area below the aircraft out to a range of around 30 miles. *Fishpond* worked by the wireless operator differentiating between the relatively slow-moving traces from the bombers around his aircraft to the faster-moving traces received from enemy fighters chasing them.

'Our bomb-aimer, Dave Hector, now found himself being given intense training to enable him to operate the H2S set whilst I received a similar kind of training

115

to enable me to use Fishpond efficiently. As the safety of the aircraft depended on my reactions I took great pains to interpret the returns displayed on the screen, asking Harry Brooker to bank the aircraft from right to left every so often so I could minutely scan the airspace below us. The bombers either side of us moved fairly slowly but fighters darting in showed up quite plainly.

Fishpond's efficacy was borne out by the use of the equipment over Karlsruhe on the night of 2/3rd February 1945 when our Lancaster, OF-H, was attacked on nine occasions by enemy nightfighters within a thirty minute time frame. By giving timely warnings of the fighter's approach, I allowed our gunners to engage them, resulting in their shooting down three of the attackers. The combat report for that flight is included in this narrative and makes for fascinating reading.

During those combats, OF-H and Harry Brooker evaded the enemy nightfighters by employing another of Cochrane's innovations, the '5 Group corkscrew', a different manoeuvre to the standard corkscrew used by other crews.'

Leslie's use of *Fishpond* and the way Harry Brooker responded to his requests to manoeuvre the aircraft in the manner described above was no doubt a major factor in their survival. By constantly weaving and banking they would have put off any nightfighter trying to draw a bead on them and it also gave Leslie a larger picture, via the *Fishpond screen*, of what was below their aircraft. Bombers flying at the same height and speed gave slower returns than a fighter screaming in to attack. The nightfighters preferred easier prey, less vigilant crews who flew straight and level for minutes at a time without keeping a proper look out, allowing the fighter to slide in below unseen and use his *Schräge Musik* guns to fatal effect.

They were left in no doubts by the squadron commander, Wing Commander Anthony Heward, that by joining 97 Squadron they were members of an elite squadron. After taking delivery of their first Lancaster on 14th January 1942 six Lancasters of 97 Sqn were sent by Air Marshall Harris on the 17th April to bomb the MAN submarine diesel factory, deep in Germany near Augsburg. It was to be a daylight raid at low level, without fighter escort and the six 97 Sqn aircraft would accompany the force leader, Squadron Leader J.D. Nettleton from 44 Squadron with his squadron's six Lancasters.

After a week's low-level training the force set off but they were attacked by German fighters just after crossing the English Channel. By the time they had passed Paris, four Lancasters had already been shot down, all of these aircraft from 44 Squadron The remainder pressed on and attacked the target with another of 44 Sqn's Lancasters being shot down attacking at chimney-top level. Two 97 Sqn Lancasters were hit by flak and exploded, OF-K piloted by Sqn Leader J.S.Sherwood DFC and OF-P flown by W/O T.J. Mycock DFC. All onboard OF-P were killed when it exploded in mid-air, among them an American serving in the RCAF, F/Sgt J.G. Donoghue.

Sqn Leader Sherwood was the only survivor from his aircraft OF-K, having a miraculous escape when he was thrown clear of the Lancaster as it crash-landed in flames near Augsburg. The remaining five aircraft made it safely back to Britain with Sqn Leader Nettleton being awarded the VC for his actions and Sherwood the DSO. The raid demonstrated once and for all that daylight attacks on Germany could only be carried out at a prohibitive cost. From now on they would attack by night and the need for special methods of marking and specially trained crews became paramount. Thus was the Pathfinder Force born.

Now flying in the Pathfinder role, 5 Group and 97 Squadron in particular were past masters in the art of 'Illuminators', lighting the target up with flares to enable the OBOE-equipped Mosquitoes to dash in at low altitude and lay their Target Indicators in a precise pattern. 97 Sqn combined a dispatch rate of fourteen-fifteen aircraft a night for most of their Pathfinder raids with a low loss rate; such was the calibre of the crews.

5 Group utilised the technique of 'Offset' marking. Markers laid down over the target were apt to be quickly extinguished by the Main Force's bombs falling on top of them, requiring the need for 'Backers-Up' to overfly the target and remark the area to be bombed. Dropping markers to the left, right, above or below the target depending on the computed wind over the target allowed the Master Bomber to give corrections over the RT to Main Force bomb aimers who adjusted their bomb-sights accordingly. The resultant fall of bombs would be in a tighter, more accurate pattern and didn't need constant remarking as the TI's were visible for longer periods than other methods.

'To be promoted to one of the 'Flare Force' positions with 97 Squadron was recognised as being amongst the best crews in Bomber Command. A scan of the operations carried out by the Brooker crew (Kaiserslautern 28th August.) shows us operating as a Flare Force III aircraft, recognition indeed.

On joining 97 Sqn our training began almost immediately. My logbook shows flight after flight of 'Y' Runs, the code for H2S training, some of these flights lasting four hours, a testament to how seriously we took to the training. The flights were flown mainly over England using English cities as aiming points to build up our experience of identifying targets in the dark and through cloud. Even London was used at one time and the Serpentine in Hyde Park showed up quite clearly through the murk. Other flights included bombing practice, fighter affiliation flights and GPI practice, the use of the H2S Ground Position Indicator in recognising landmarks below our aircraft. On one bombing practice run we achieved an impressive accuracy of 42yds from 20,000ft.

We completed only two operations in September and none in October, bad weather playing a major factor in the latter part of the year. Being a specialist marker squadron meant we were only required when conditions were conducive to our type of operations. Most of October's log book entries are down to more training as we were driven hard to ensure we were up to the stringent requirements the CO demanded of his crews.

We'd gather in Coningsby's distinct Briefing Room to discover where we'd be flying to that night. It had posters all round the walls, a large blackboard that was the aircraft status board and a cover over the map of Europe that designated the target. The chairs were hard, foldaway wooden affairs that soon made your backside numb as you struggled to concentrate. It crossed my mind more than once that perhaps the sadist who designed the chairs had that effect uppermost in his mind, a handy method of keeping tired crews awake long enough to take in all the information they needed for the forthcoming operation.

Daylight raids were now over as we trained hard for the task of night-marking. In the future, the only sight we'd see beneath us piercing the darkness would be the nightmare winking of incendiaries burning brightly *against the pressure waves of 4,000lb 'cookies' radiating outwards, and the brightly-coloured Target Indicators we'd dropped. The Germans called our TI's 'Christmas Trees', from the bright, tinselly glare they gave off as they descended. Set against all this would be flame-tipped bursts of flak and slow-burning parachute flares dropped by enemy nightfighters as they prowled the perimeter of the target area looking for easy prey.*

Someone once asked me how we felt on completing an operation and I answered that my one abiding memory was one of relief as we exited the target area. A sense of elation would set in and some crew members would cheer over the intercom before Harry Brooker restored discipline and we settled down to the rigours of the return flight to Coningsby.

What about feelings of guilt? None that I could remember, it was an exceptional time in all of our lives and the feeling was that there was a job to do and until it was finished we would fly until one side or the other surrendered. It was an experience that I would not like to repeat and looking back now after sixty-five years the months of operational flying have assumed a dim and distant trace in my memory.'

In a sense, Leslie and his fellow crew members started their operational flying at a time when the German nightfighter force had peaked. From its zenith in the autumn of 1943 losses to the nightfighters had steadily declined, reaching a low of 0.7% in December 1944. Although, strength-wise, most nightfighter *Gruppen* still possessed aircraft and aircrew in numbers, technology had overtaken them. *Freya* and *Würzburg* ground-based radars and *Lichtenstein SN-2* the fighter's airborne radar had been jammed since August 1944. Other airborne detection systems such as *Naxos* and *Flensburg* had been nullified by the bombers turning off their *Monica* and *H2S* radars at intervals during their approach to the target, before *Monica* was removed altogether.

Gone were the days when the German ground listening services could detect the allied aircraft tuning their radios prior to take-off, thus providing an early warning of an impending raid. Now, in August 1944, *Mandrel*-equipped RAF aircraft prowled the allied-occupied areas jamming the Ground Control Radars and listening services. The bomber stream frequently split into two or even three parts and attacked from different directions, causing the fighters to be sent to different parts of the Reich not threatened. Diversionary raids also took the fighters away from the Main Force and it was a lucky day when all the nightfighter force could be vectored by radio onto the main weight of the bomber stream.

German-speaking operators, transmitting from Britain, gave confusing voice commands over the radio, contradicting the real German controllers. When the Germans brought in women to do the job the British responded very quickly by bringing in their own women who continued the airborne harassment. Microphones placed in engine nacelles transmitted on fighter frequencies and drowned out commands over the air, adding to the confusion felt by the hunters.

That is not to say heavy losses still didn't occur. When the German ground controllers got it right and a fair numbers of nightfighters could engage the bomber stream heavy losses could and did occur, even in the dying days of the war. From January to April of 1945, German nightfighters shot down 529 aircraft, most of them four-engined bombers. On the night of 24/25th February 1945 24 aircraft were lost, one of them a 97 Sqn aircraft, OF-E, flown by F/L J.B Hines on a raid to Oslo Fiord. The Lancaster was shot down after exchanging fire with a

Ju88 nightfighter, all but one of the crew's bodies being recovered and buried in Tonsberg Cemetery, Norway.

Fortunately, Harry Brooker and his crew were not airborne that night but the loss of eight of their comrades served to remind Leslie and his fellow crew members that the war still had a course to run before the final victory.

The bomber stream itself now flew at lower altitudes, confusing any enemy fighter lucky to have an operational radar onboard as the bomber was frequently lost in the ground return 'clutter' from the bomber's practise of dispensing 'Window' strips at regular intervals. Only the Master Bombers tended to fly high over the target and the Germans tried to intercept them without much real success.

Below is a description of the 24 raids Harry Brooker and his crew carried out with 97 Squadron and events surrounding them during their operational flying. Where possible, the narrative for each 'op' has been taken from 97 Squadron's Operations Log and the follow-up description below in italics taken from Bomber Command's Campaign diaries. 97 Squadron flew a total of 4,091 sorties during the war, losing 130 aircraft. The squadron's operational markings were OF-. All the aircraft Harry Brooker and his crew flew in on Pathfinder raids were Lancaster Mk. III's with the uprated Merlin 338 engines.

The first casualty suffered by 97 Sqn after the Brooker crew's arrival occurred on the night of 11/12th September 1944, when OF-Q, registration PB510, was lost on an operation to Darmstadt. The pilot, S/L H.R. A. De Belleroche and two of his crew, Sgt. W.J. Parsons and F/Sgt W.W. Winskill RCAF survived to become POW's, the remainder of their crew being killed. A grim reminder to Leslie and his friends of the deadly game they were all players in.

Bomb loads carried by the Pathfinders comprised mainly of flares and Target Indicators, although as can be seen sometimes heavier bombs were carried in addition to the marking pyrotechnics. 'Clusters' were the flares carried for illumination and the Target Indicators (TI's) came in two main colours, red or green. The Germans were adept in copying these to lure the Main Force to bomb open countryside hence the need for the Master Bomber to keep a close eye on what was being dropped, and where.

'A week later, our crew climbed into Lancaster III OF-E for our first operational raid with 97 Sqn. All the weeks of training now came down to the actions we would carry out in the following hours. No easy flight over the Channel to attack a flying bomb in daylight where we could see the dangers, this operation would signify our baptism of fire at night as a Pathfinder Marker aircraft laying down flares for the Main Force to bomb on.

Fear, trepidation but above all, a fierce determination to do the job satisfactorily and come home again was in our minds as we set off.'

15. 19/20th September 1944. Mönchengladbach (Rheydt.).

OF-E. ND862. F/L H.Brooker, Sgt W.J.Morgan, F/O K.Brown, Sgts D.Hector, **L.Smith**, F/Sgt P.Rainsford, F/Sgt W.Lieberman. Up 1919 down 2331. 12x7" clusters, 2x1000lb MC (½hr delay.) Clear, good visibility. Target confirmed on H2S. On first run over target, illumination considered sufficient so decided to drop our two bombs only-blind as briefed. Orbited awaiting instructions, when Controller asked for more flares: we went straight in and dropped 6 with flash. No markers down before our flares, but we saw red TI cascading as we left target. Controller called in Main Force and told them to bomb red TI with overshoot as planned. All markers and flare droppers then told to go home.

227 Lancasters and 10 Mosquitoes of No's 1 and No 5 Groups to the twin towns of Mönchengladbach/Rheydt. 4 Lancasters and 1 Mosquito lost. Bomber Command claimed severe damage to both towns, particularly to Mönchengladbach.

The Master Bomber for this raid was <u>Wing Commander Guy Gibson</u>*, VC, DSO, DFC flying a No 627 Squadron Mosquito from Coningsby, where he was serving as Base Operations Officer. Gibson's instructions over the target were heard throughout the raid and gave no hint of trouble, but his aircraft crashed in flames - according to a Dutch eyewitness - before crossing the coast of Holland for the homeward flight over the North Sea. There were no German fighter claims for the Mosquito; it may have been damaged by flak over the target or on the return flight, or it may have developed engine trouble. It was possibly flying too low for the crew to escape by parachute. Gibson and his navigator, Squadron Leader JB Warwick DFC, were both killed and were buried in the Roman Catholic Cemetery at Steenbergen-en-Kruisland, 13km north of Bergen-op-Zoom. Theirs are the only graves of Allied servicemen in the cemetery.*

Sqn Leader Warwick was a two-tour expired navigator who was serving as the Coningsby Base Navigation Officer at the time of his death. He did not have to fly operations but volunteered to crew up with Wing Commander Gibson, who had been allowed by AOC Arthur Harris to fly this one last operation before being permanently grounded after completing 177 operations.

For the operation over Mönchengladbach, Gibson 'borrowed' a Mosquito. He'd only had one flight in a 'Mossie', Warwick had never flown in one before. A theory has since been put forward that unfamiliarity caused Mosquito KB267, AZ-E's crash in that the crew failed to change the fuel tanks over via the fuel selector valve and the engines simply stopped due to fuel starvation.

Gibson's last words over the radio were, 'Nice work, chaps, now beat it home.' and after that, silence. It was said that the AOC of 5 Group, AVM Sir Ralph Cochrane, waited at Coningsby for the returning 97 Sqn crews, asking each of them if anyone had heard from Gibson after leaving the target.

At the same time that Harry Brooker and Leslie exited their aircraft, glad to have their first pathfinder operation over safely, further down the dispersal Canadian pilot, F/L George Laing DFC and Bar and his crew were holding a different sort of celebration. The Monchengladbach raid was their last, their fiftieth 'op' in a double tour of thirty with 57 Sqn and twenty with 97 Sqn. Whilst the Brooker crew had more night operations to contemplate, George Laing's crew had fourteen days well-earned leave and a stand-down from operations for the rest of the war.

97 Squadron were detailed for a raid on 23/24th September on an aqueduct near the German town of Münster. Harry Brooker's crew did not participate in this raid but two 97 Sqn aircraft were lost, Squadron Leader R.M. Higgs DFC in OF-F and Flying Officer Lopez RAAF in OF-B.

Lancaster OF-F crashed at 2340hrs near the town of Burgsteinfurt and only W/O H.S.Tiller DFM RAAF survived to become a POW. OF-B crashed into the North Sea in the early hours of 24th September off Heacham, Norfolk, killing the entire crew. Their bodies were eventually washed ashore in the following weeks and taken for burial. Also lost the same night, attacking the same target, were three Lancasters from 61 Squadron. Two of those lost were aircraft Leslie and the crew had flown operations in the previous month, being QR-E and QR-W. QR-E was shot down over Wechte, Germany with only one survivor, Sgt H.Lea whilst QR-W crashed into the River Waal in Holland with only one survivor also, Sgt J.G. Miller.

61 Squadron had lost another aircraft earlier the same day when QR-T was shot down by flak and crashed into the sea off Calais. By an amazing coincidence, QR-T was yet another of the aircraft Leslie had flown in, making it three out of the four aircraft lost that day by 61 Sqn that the Brooker crew had previously flown with. There were two survivors from QR-T, F/Sgt D.Gordon and F/Sgt P.D. Cook.

Not for the last time fate had smiled on Harry Brooker and his crew. There was a distinct possibility that had they stayed with 61 Sqn it could have been them in one of the four aircraft lost on 24th May 1944 and this story would have been stillborn.

16. 26/27th September 1944.Karlsruhe.

OF-K. JA846. F/L H. Brooker, Sgt W.J.Morgan, F/Sgt K.Mannion, F/O K.Brown, Sgts. D.Hector (A/B2), **L.Smith**, W.Hunter, A. D'Arcy. Up 0057 down 0704. 12x7" clusters, 2xTI green No.16, 1 rec flare.10/10ths cloud. Target located by existing flares and cascading TI's-seen to burst on approach. Ran over target area but did not drop as glow difficult to distinguish. Heard Controller order us to back up concentration of reds and greens.

226 Lancasters and 11 Mosquitoes of No's 1 and No 5 Groups to Karlsruhe. 2 Lancasters lost. Bomber Command claimed a concentrated attack, with a large area of the city devastated.

97 Squadron Log claims the raid on Karlsruhe was a failure due to cloud conditions and searchlights making accurate bombing impossible. The flak was heavy and although a few nightfighters were seen no squadron aircraft were lost. It was also a reason for F/Sgt Reg Powell DFM to celebrate as his tour came to an end, having completed 45 operations.

17.   27/28th September 1944. Kaiserslautern.
OF-E. ND862. F/L H.Brooker, Sgt W.Morgan, F/O K.Brown, Sgts D.J. Hector, **L.Smith**, W.Hunter, A. D'Arcy. Up 2155 down 0441. 9x7″ clusters, 2xTI red No 16. 3x 1000lb MC (1/2 hour delay.) 2 rec flares. Clear below 8,000ft. Identified target visually in light of flares. As we were Flare Force III, our flares and TI's had not to be dropped unless called for. Dropped bombs as instructed. First flares were excellent and town clearly seen. Main Force called in to bomb at 0058 hrs and the bombing seemed very concentrated.

217 Lancasters and 10 Mosquitoes of No's 1 and 5 Groups in the only major raid carried out by Bomber Command during the war, on Kaiserslautern. 1 Lancaster and 1 Mosquito lost.

On the 10th October 1944. Wing Commander Heward DFC AFC relinquished command of 97 Squadron and handed over the reins to Group Captain P.W. Johnson DFC AFC who carried out his first operation with his new squadron on 1st November when four Lancasters took part in a raid on Hamburg. During the month of October 97 Squadron carried out only five operations, the rest of the month being spent in flying training and practise bombing. The Brooker crew participated in none of the five operations, concentrating on their Marker training.

18.   6th November 1944. Gravenhorst. (Ems-Weser canal.)

OF-D. PB450. F/L H.L. Brooker. Sgt W. Morgan, F/O K.Brown, F/Sgt D.J.Hector, F/O J.A. Pearce (AB2), Sgts **L.Smith**, A. D'Arcy, F/L A.H. Jones.   Up 1646 down 2117. 6x7" clusters, 2 reco flares. Clear, no haze. Located target visually on green TI's and flares. Saw green TI's at about 1919hrs. First green TI appeared accurate but second was some miles to west of number 1. First flares appeared accurate. No reds seen at 1924 or 1925 hrs. A marker aircraft was heard to ask Controller for more flares to the east. Routemarker not seen.

235 Lancasters and 7 Mosquitoes of No 5 Group attempted to cut the Mittelland Canal at its junction with the Dortmund-Ems Canal at Gravenhorst. The marking force experienced great difficulty in finding the target. The crew of a low-flying Mosquito - pilot: Flight Lieutenant LCE De Vigne; navigator: Australian Squadron Leader FW Boyle, No 627 Squadron - found the canal and dropped their marker with such accuracy that it fell into the water and was extinguished. Only 31 aircraft bombed, before the Master Bomber ordered the raid to be abandoned. 10 Lancasters were lost.

On the evening of the 6th, besides 15 aircraft sent to Gravenhorst, another 6 Lancasters of 97 Squadron attacked Rheine as 'Supporter' flare markers. Slight flak and much nightfighter activity was reported but all aircraft returned safely although many diverted to other stations owing to fog, OF-K piloted by F/O W.J. Greening crash-landed at Snetterton Heath. All the crew survived but the aircraft, ND692, must have been written off as the Brooker crew flew in another squadron aircraft with the markings OF-K in January 1945, this particular Lancaster's registration being PB905.

On the night of the 10th November, six 97 Sqn aircraft took part in a cross-country exercise over France involving the aircraft's LORAN navigational equipment, an American navigational system that had been fitted to several aircraft. The exercise involved flying close to the French-German border and it was here that events unravelled.

Two aircraft failed to return and a third was badly shot–up by enemy flak. OF-D, registration PB450, and its entire crew, flown by one of the squadron's most promising pilots, F/L J.S.Runnancles, disappeared without a trace. The other aircraft, OF-G, PB200, flown by F/O C.E. T. Peters dived into marshy ground near the French village of Cernay-en-Dormois at 2225 hrs killing all its crew. It is possible OF-G fell victim to a marauding nightfighter but the aircraft was completely burnt out and left nothing but a 15ft deep crater in the marshy surroundings. Two of the most experienced LORAN operators in the squadron were lost, one in each aircraft and as a result no more LORAN training flights were carried out over enemy territory.

19. 22/23rd November 1944. Trondheim.

OF-P. ED862. F/L H.Brooker, Sgt W.Morgan, F/O K.Brown, F/Sgt D.J.Hector, F/O J.A.Pearce (AB2) Sgts **L.Smith**, A. D'Arcy, F/L A.H. Jones. Up 1557 down 0209. 14 Cp No3 Mk II 2 rec flares. Clear. Target identified visually by ground detail. 2 green TI's seen 3 miles west of target. Flares scattered.

22/23rd November 1944. 171 Lancasters and 7 Mosquitoes of 5 Group were dispatched to attack the U-Boat pens at Trondheim but the target was covered by a smoke-screen and the Master

Bomber ordered the raid to be abandoned after the illuminating force and marking force had been unable to find the target. 2 Lancasters and 1 Mosquito lost.

18 aircraft from 97 Squadron, Harry Brooker and his crew included, took part in the raid on Trondheim. All returned safely but OF-L suffered an engine failure on the return leg, landing safely on three engines. All the Main Force aircraft returned with the bombs still onboard, a long, tiring flight with nothing to show for the three aircraft lost. It was also one of their pilots, F/L D.Shorter's last operation, having reached the magical figure of 45 operations and he departed a week later for a well-earned rest,

20. 4/5th December 1944. Heilbronn.

OF-E. PB588. F/L H.L.Brooker, Sgt W.J.Morgan, F/O K.Brown, F/S D.J. Hector, F/O J.A.Pearce (NZ) **Sgt L. Smith**, F/L A.H.Jones, Sgt A. D'Arcy. Up 1610 down 2241. 14CP No.1. Clear sky, good visibility. Target identified by existing flares, river and built-up area. 1st Red T.I was down before we dropped and was dead accurate. It was backed up almost immediately. 1st Green was seen to explode but died out. 2nd Green T.I seen to be on target area at approx 1919hrs. Assessment not heard on VHF. Link 4 heard at H-17 approx apart from this nothing heard. At H-20 wind sent was 292/54. Average wind from Lancs was 284/57. Link 1 transmitted same wind , we did not therefore transmit ours. Suspected smoke screen seen to North of Heckeraum during beginning of attack to East and West of river.

Heilbronn: 282 Lancasters and 10 Mosquitoes of No 5 Group. 12 Lancasters lost. This was a crushing blow on Heilbronn which stood on a main north-south railway line but was

otherwise of little importance. It was the first and only major raid by Bomber Command on this target. 1,254 tons of bombs fell in a few minutes and the post-war British Bombing Survey Unit estimated that 351 acres, 82 per cent of the town's built-up area, were destroyed, mainly by fire. Much investigation by various people resulted in the reliable estimate that just over 7,000 people died. Most of these victims would have died in fires so intense that there was probably a genuine firestorm.

The 16 Lancasters of 97 Sqn who reached Heilbronn marked the target in clear skies using their H2S sets so well that the Main Force were able to deliver a crushing attack which devastated the town.

21. 6/7ᵗʰ December 1944. Giessen.

OF-H. PB700. F/L H.L.Brooker, Sgt W.J.Morgan, F/O K.Brown, F/S D.J.Hector, F/O J.A.Pearce (Visual B/A. NZ), **Sgt L.B.Smith**, F/L A.H.Jones, Sgt A.D'Arcy. Up 1702 down 2305. 14 CpNo.3. Clear: visibility good, thin cloud to W. Target identified visually by Green T.I. Flare Force I appeared to drop their flares short, so we dropped ours visually on Green T.I which was in built-up area. No flare seemed to illuminate built-up area before we dropped. First Red backed up by three others, forming good cluster. First Red fell about 1 min after we dropped.

Giessen: 255 Lancasters and 10 Mosquitoes of No 5 Group. 8 Lancasters lost. There were two aiming points for this raid. 168 aircraft were allocated to the town centre and 87 to the railway yards. Severe damage was caused at both places.

That the nightfighters were not yet a spent force was highlighted by the numerous 97 Sqn aircraft who reported combats near and returning from the target area. OF-M flown by F/O Yaxley was shot up by an Me410 and his

Mid-Upper gunner, Sgt Wilkinson injured. During the fight OF-M's gunners managed to shoot down a Ju88 despite their port outer engine having to be shut down due to enemy shell damage. All aircraft returned safely.

On the 8th, the first snows of the winter fell and the weather precluded any flying operations. An operation was planned for the 9/10th but after the ten aircraft despatched had taken off they were recalled whilst over the Thames Estuary due to bad weather over the intended target.

22. 13/14th December 1944. Oslo Fjord.
OF-C. PB133. F/L H.L.Brooker, Sgt W.J.Morgan, F/O K.Brown, F/Sgt D.J.Hector, F/O J.A.Pearce (Visual B/A. NZ), **Sgt L.B.Smith**, F/L A.H.Jones, Sgt A.D'Arcy. Up 1534 down 2255 (Milltown). 9CP No.3, 5x1000MC. Clear. Identified target on H2S, confirmed visually. Dropped flares blind as briefed. Orbited Port, came round on heading 145 after losing 4,000ft. Controller said ship was lit up well. Came in and bombed as planned at approx 1900hrs. Saw a ship in approx position as briefed (East of headland) Ship obscured by smoke in later stages of bombing run, so aimed at smoke.

52 Lancasters and 7 Mosquitoes of No 5 Group were sent to attack the German cruiser Koln berthed in Oslo Fjord but, when the bombers reached Oslo Fjord, the Koln had moved to another location. Other ships were bombed instead but the results were not observed. No aircraft lost.

The targets 97 Sqn were to mark were the German cruisers, Emden and Köln which were berthed in Oslo harbour. 14 aircraft took off in poor visibility for the long flight over to Norway. The attack was carried out with no results seen and on return the crews diverted to Leslie's favourite airbase in Scotland, Milltown near Lossiemouth. Poor weather kept them there until the late afternoon when they took off and returned to Coningsby and to some decent food!

23. 17/18ᵗʰ December 1944. Munich.

OF-Q. PB521. F/L H.L. Brooker, Sgt W.J.Morgan, F/O K.Brown, F/S D.J. Hector, F/O J.A. Pearce (Vis B/A. NZ), **Sgt L.B.Smith**, F/L A.H. Jones, Sgt A.D'Arcy. Up 1623 down 0126. 14 Cp No.1. Clear. Good visibility. Target identified by Green T.I's and flares. H2S u/s after 08.00E obliged to drop flares visually but on same heading as briefed. First Red T.I fell accurately on Northern tip of latticed oval; assessed, and main force called in before H-hour. One Green T.I was badly out and one stick of flares fell nearly 6 miles West, just before we bombed. Some good explosions later. Incendiary concentration good; slight undershoot of some. Much activity in marshalling yards. Difficulty in climbing. Marking very efficient. Bombing good.

Munich: 280 Lancasters and 8 Mosquitoes of No 5 Group. 4 Lancasters lost. Bomber Command claimed 'severe and widespread damage' in the old centre of Munich and at railway targets.

14 crews of 97 Sqn marked the city of Munich with all returning safely. The green TI's were seen to land squarely in the midst of the built-up area of the city and the resulting bombing caused large fires to break out. For three men of 97 Sqn, it was their final op, the fact causing hope amongst the other crews that now they too could see the war out.

24. 18/19th December 1944. Gdynia.

OF-A. PA973. F/L H.L.Brooker, Sgt W.J.Morgan, F/O K.Brown, F/Sgt D.J.Hector, F/O J.A.Pearce (Vis B/A. NZ) **F/Sgt L.B. Smith,** F/L A.H.Jones, Sgt A.D'Arcy. Up 1715 down 0236. 1 Green T.I, B.25, 13xCP No.3. Clear; visibility good. Located target by H2S. Two Yellow T.I's seen in corner between No's 3 and 4 docks, none in the marshalling yard. We had good run and dropped on time. Illumination from flares very good. Red and Green T.I's were in position as briefed. Three only seen to cascade; the other two burst on hitting ground. Order given to bomb S.W Red T.I with vector wind as planned. Marker III called in to back up the Red T.I. Marking was excellent.

236 Lancasters of No 5 Group attacked the distant port of Gdynia on the Baltic coast and caused damage to shipping, installations and housing in the port area. 4 Lancasters lost.

A nine-hour return flight to Gdynia saw all 97 Sqn's 15 aircraft return safely. The port stood out starkly against the backdrop of heavy snow and marking was carried out successfully, causing much damage from the Main Force's bombs. Leslie's rank on this op was incorrectly given as that of Flight Sergeant in the Squadron's Operations Log.

25. 21/22nd December 1944. Politz (Stettin.).

OF-A. PA973. F/L H.L.Brooker, Sgt W.J.Morgan, F/O K.Brown, F/Sgt D.J.Hector, F/O J.A.Pearce (Visual B/A.NZ) **Sgt. L.B.Smith,** F/L A.H.Jones, Sgt A.D'Arcy. Up 1638 down 0239. 14xCP No.3. Clear. Target identified on H2S. Dropped 14 flares blind. Marker 1 marked immediately as we finished our run; this was assessed as being 200yds from target. Large explosion at 2205hrs.

Decoy fire site seen in action. Controller warned force of this at H-11.

207 Lancasters and 1 Mosquito of No 5 Group attacked the synthetic-oil refinery at Politz, near Stettin. 3 Lancasters were lost** and 5 more crashed in England. Post-raid reconnaissance showed that the power-station chimneys had collapsed and that other parts of the plant were damaged.

Lancaster OF-M, Registration PB461, flown by F/O Sinclair RAAF was the last 97 Sqn aircraft to be lost in 1944. It crashed in Norway on the return trip from Politz, with no survivors. Five aircraft landed away at Wick and Gp Capt Johnson landed at Metheringham owing to bad weather on return. It had been a gruelling flight with most aircraft airborne for almost ten hours.

On the 25th December, in a thick fog and white frost, the squadron was stood down from operations and all the NCO's and squadron officers attended the Airmen's Christmas Dinner, a welcome break.

Only two more operations were carried out by squadron aircraft during the last days of 1944, two operations to Horten to find and bomb German cruisers. Leslie's crew was not called on and all the aircraft detailed on these raids returned safely.

Included in the December 1944 reports contained within 97 Squadron's Operation Logbook are the following awards:

*F/O K.Brown and **Sgt. L.B. Smith** Temporary award of the Pathfinder Badge.*

'Between raids we carried out practice bombing flights, fighter affiliation to practise the methods available for avoiding enemy fighters, attended

lectures and were driven hard by Wing Commander Baker to improve our bombing technique. Known as a 'bastard,' W/C Baker was a hard taskmaster but the lessons he imbued stood us in good stead as our tally of 'op's increased and we felt our slight chances of surviving a tour improving.'

The strain of flying on operations was immense and many aircrew buckled under the relentless pressure. Some people have a fear of flying which is quite normal but it was the fear of *operational* flying that was to test many men to the limit. Everyone is born with an inbuilt sense of courage but some have a deeper reservoir than others and it was this depth that was to be sorely tested during the months of a tour.

The RAF's response to anyone flagging was brutal and immediate. The so-called 'cowards' were swiftly removed from flying duties and publicly humiliated by having their aircrew brevets ripped from their tunics before being sent from the camp to menial duties elsewhere.

'This was savagely brought home to me and my fellow crew members when on our return from one raid the mid-upper gunner, Paddy, lost his nerve after the aircraft was bracketed by flak. As we crossed the Dutch coast on the homeward leg a flak shell exploded opposite Paddy's turret causing minor damage and injuring him slightly. The experience caused him to become hysterical, he began screaming to be let out and had to be tranquillised before we landed. All the strain of the five months spent on operations came to a head and he suffered a mental collapse.

On landing he was removed to be swiftly charged with LMF ie 'Lack of Moral Fibre', a catch-all phrase aimed at those whose reservoir had hit rock bottom

136

and could not continue flying. A short time later we were ordered to one of the most ignoble parades ever. From Coningsby we were taken to nearby Woodhall Spa and with the rest of 5 Group made to watch Paddy and a few other unfortunates have their Court Martial sentences read out. These men then suffered the humiliation of having their sergeant's stripes and aircrew brevets wrenched from their uniforms before capless and bare-headed they were marched away to the air station gates to the roll of accompanying drums.

After having 'spare bods' fly with us for a few operations as a replacement gunner, Paddy's place in the mid-upper turret was taken up by Flt/Lt Albert Jones, a former Dance Instructor at the Hammersmith Palais in London.

Ironically, I was to meet up with Paddy in the Flying Horse pub in Nottingham a few months later. Sitting before us in 'civvies' sipping Ansells Ale, he regaled us with a tale of how he'd procured a safe job as an inspector of aircraft turrets with Boulton-Paul on wages which made us turn green with envy. Such is fate!'

Although the authorities reacted harshly to anyone flagging, they did recognise the strain of flying on operations which is why so many of the aircrew's Mess drinking binges and escapades were excused under the umbrella of 'high spirits.' The mental adjustment required when taking off from a tranquil British countryside, arriving over a hostile environment where to linger meant death and then return only hours later to that same undisturbed, tranquil British countryside, was immense. Leave was one of the remedies used to ensure men had the opportunity to relax away from base and was frequently granted on the basis of ten days for every six weeks spent on operations.

Leslie travelled to London every time he was granted leave and took the overnight train from King's Cross to Aberdeen. From there he travelled on to Ardersier and his relative's farm and the air war could take on a distant aspect as he visited his mother at Fort George.

The war did not stop for the festive period. 97 Squadron ushered in the New Year with raids on the 1st January, splitting their strength and operating against Ladbergen and the Dortmund-Ems Canal. Further raids followed to Royan (4/5th.) and a 'Gardening' exercise (6/7th), mine-laying off the enemy coast where they released the mines by use of their H2S sets. No Sqn aircraft were lost and it was not until the night of the 7/8th that Leslie and his fellow crew members boarded their aircraft, OF-C, as they prepared to raid the very heart of the Reich, Munich.

26. 7/8th January 1945. Munich.
OF-E. PB133. F/L H.L.Brooker, Sgt W. Morgan, F/O K.Brown, F/Sgt D.J.Hector, F/O J.A. Pearce (Vis AB), **Sgt L.Smith**, F/Sgt A.Rainsford, F/Sgt W.Liebermann. Up 1713 down 0135. 6x1000lb TI green, 5x250lb TI green. Hazy, some cloud at 18,000ft and above. Visual location of target on red TI. Two red TI's were seen on side of river with the bridge at the centre. Our TI's were aimed at the actual M/P which was clearly visible by the light of the flares, those being in good concentration. The flashing "V" and the greens were clearly visible. Wind found 300/35 passed to Link I at 2017 hrs. Route marker dropped in position as briefed 2121hrs, 18,000ft.

645 Lancasters and 9 Mosquitoes of No's 1, 3, 5, 6 and 8 Groups to Munich. 11 Lancasters lost and 4 more crashed in

France. Bomber Command claimed a successful area raid, with the central and some industrial areas being severely damaged. This was the last major raid on Munich.

27. 14/15<u>th</u> January 1945. Merseburg. (Leuna Oil Plant.)

OF-K. PB905. F/L H. L. Brooker, Sgt W.Morgan, F/O K.Brown, F/Sgt D.J. Hector F/O J. A. Pearce (Vis AB), **Sgt L.Smith**, W/O H. J. Silzer, F/Sgt A. D'Arcy. Up 1614 down 0157 (At Breighton.) 14xCP No 3. Hazy: target identified visually. Dropped flares then stood by as we were Link 1 but we could not transmit on VHF as "Press to Speak" plug had come out. Passed bombing wind 040/129 at H-7, H-5 and H-3 on W/T. At H-2 handed over to Link III. First red went down at 2045hrs and they continued to go down all through the attack. Very scattered except for about 3 or 4 which were very close to the M/P.

573 Lancasters and 14 Mosquitoes of No's 1, 5, 6 and 8 Groups carried out two attacks, 3 hours apart, on the synthetic oil plant at Leuna. The attacks caused severe damage throughout the plant. Albert Speer, in his post-war interrogations, stated that this was one of a group of most damaging raids on the synthetic-oil industry carried out during this period. 10 Lancasters lost.

This was a deep-penetration raid carried out successfully by the 14 crews from 97 Sqn involved. The Flare Force to which Harry Brooker's crew belonged, marked the target sufficiently well to allow the Mosquitoes to drop down and place their marker flares in exactly the right spot, causing wide-spread damage. Fog over Lincolnshire meant a diversion to RAF Breighton on their return from another nine-hour flight, all aircraft landing safely.

28. 16/17th January 1945. Brux.

OF-K. PB905. F/L H. L. Brooker, Sgt W. Morgan, F/O K. Brown, F/Sgt D.J.Hector, F/O J.A.Pearce (Vis AB) **Sgt L.Smith**, F/L A.H.Jones, Sgt D'Arcy. Up 1805 down 0234. 11xCP No 3, 3x1,000lb TI green. 10/10ths low cloud, tops about 5,000ft. Reached target on time. Neither VBU nor Flare Force 3 required. Green TI was seen to go down and showed well enough to bomb on. Emergency marking got smothered quickly in cloud but visible glare remained from the TI. There was a mushroom of smoke over the target and on return we saw a big blueish explosion lighting up the sky at 2307 hrs. Landed at Hulme.

231 Lancasters and 6 Mosquitoes of No's 1 and No 5 Groups attacked a synthetic-oil plant at Brüx in Western Czechoslovakia. The raid was a complete success. Speer also mentioned this raid as causing a particularly severe setback to oil production. 1 Lancaster lost.

15 aircraft from 97 Sqn provided the marking for this attack, with the CO, Group Captain Johnson, assuming the airborne role of Deputy Controller over the target. Because of thick cloud obscuring the target the marker aircraft dropped sky markers to great effect and accurate bombing from the Main Force caused widespread damage. More fog over Lincolnshire meant a diversion to RAF Hulme for Leslie and the crew.

29. 1st February 1945. Siegen.

OF-H. PB700. F/L H.L. Brooker, Sgt W. Morgan, F/L K. Brown, F/Sgt D.J. Hector, F/L J.A.Pearce (Vis AB) **F/Sgt L.B Smith**, F/L A.H. Jones, F/Sgt W.D.Noall. Up 1559 down 2159. 12xCP No1, 2X250lb TI green. 10/10ths cloud, base 3,000ft, tops 5,000ft. Target identified on H2S. We dropped our flares on time and as briefed. Orbited awaiting emergency method order and after Main Force commenced bombing concentration of red TI's, we called Controller and asked if this method was required at 1921hrs. He replied that this was not necessary and that we could go home.

Siegen: 271 Lancasters and 11 Mosquitoes of No 5 Group. 3 Lancasters and 1 Mosquito lost. This raid also experienced difficult marking and bombing conditions. Some damage was caused to the railway station but the local report says that the markers were either carried away from Siegen by a strong wind or that dummy markers and a decoy fire site attracted much of the bombing. Most of the raid fell in country areas outside Siegen.

The Allies launched an air offensive named 'Clarion' on the 2nd February whose declared aim was the total destruction of the German communications network. For eight days thousands of tons of bombs were dropped on Germany round the clock, the towns of Duisburg, Worms and Karlsruhe suffering from 1,000-bomber raids during that time. The German nightfighters rose to meet the challenge, top ace Major Schnaufer of NJG4 scoring nine victories in one 24 hour period. Leslie and his crew would experience their efforts one night over Karlsruhe. Over Worms, eight nightfighter crews shot down 21 bombers in half an hour. Karlsruhe that same night also saw the nightfighters out in force, both over the target area and on the return route, and it was only Leslie's timely intervention that saved the aircraft and crew.

30. 2/3rd February 1945 – Karlsruhe.

OF-H. PB700. F/L H.L.Brooker, Sgt W.J.Morgan, F/L K.Brown, F/Sgt D.J.Hector, F/L J.A.Pearce (Vis AB), **F/Sgt L.B.Smith**, F/L A.H.Jones, F/Sgt W.D.Noall. Up 2003 Down 0255. 2 x 250lb TI green, 12 CP No 1. 10/10ths cloud. Target located by H2S. Owing to Gee and Loran being u/s early in the trip, target was reached too late to drop our flares. We carried out Controller's instructions and dropped our emergency greens. After leaving target we were attacked almost continually from 2321 hrs to 2350 hrs by enemy fighters. At 2206 hrs at position 4940N 0500E 18,000', there was a large explosion under cloud, followed by red glow, believed to be collision. We claimed one Me410 and one Ju88 destroyed, and another Me410 as a probable as it was seen with one wing on fire.

Combat Report for OF-H.

Lancaster OF–H PB700 2321 hrs 16,000' 4855N 0825E Target area on track. No moon. Clear. 10/10ths cloud below. Visibility good owing to flares under cloud.

Aircraft was just starting homeward in target area. Rear gunner (F/Sgt Noall) saw an Me410 starboard quarter down. This aircraft had a cupola with 2 upward firing guns elevated about 60/70 degrees from horizontal. Immediate combat manoeuvre was given of corkscrew starboard and the rear gunner fired a long burst at 500 yards. The enemy aircraft moved to port quarter up. The Mid Upper (F/L Jones) opened fire with a long burst and a small ball of flame appeared under the fuselage, but the enemy aircraft still came in. The mid upper fired another very long burst and the enemy aircraft just blew to pieces in the air. The explosion was seen by both gunners, the pilot and the Engineer.

At 2326 hrs 12,000' – an aircraft was seen on Fishpond. It was then picked up by the rear gunner and identified as an Me109. Evasive action was taken and the enemy aircraft disappeared. No rounds fired. Immediately after another enemy aircraft was picked up on Fishpond. It was then picked up by the rear gunner and then the mid upper gunner. It was identified as an Me 109. Perhaps the same as in previous attack. Evasive action was taken and enemy aircraft disappeared. No rounds fired owing to patches of cloud.

At 2330 hrs 7000' – Mid upper gunner saw a JU88 crossing from port to starboard slightly down. Mid upper warned rear gunner who picked it up immediately. Enemy aircraft turned in to attack from starboard quarter down and rear gunner gave corkscrew starboard. Rear gunner fired two long bursts. Enemy aircraft came up dead astern level. Both gunners fired a long burst. Enemy aircraft went out of sight of mid upper gunner behind the tail. Rear gunner then fired two more very long bursts. The enemy aircraft was then seen to dive vertically downwards, it crashed on the ground and exploded and burst on the ground. It was seen by pilot, engineer and both gunners still burning on the ground.

At 2332 hrs an aircraft was seen on Fishpond. Evasive action taken. Pilot called "Can you see it rear gunner?" There was no reply. Mid upper called up rear gunner. Still no reply. Pilot again called up rear gunner without answer so he ordered the Navigator to go back and investigate. Mid upper now saw the enemy aircraft (a JU88 dead astern) and altered the evasive action and the enemy aircraft was lost to his view under the fuselage. This enemy aircraft fired bursts of trace which went over top of OF–H. Mid upper called out "I have lost it, keep corkscrewing". Then from the tail, the rear gunner called out "OK, I've got it". Cloud was very patchy here and the fighter was lost. Pilot asked rear gunner what had happened and rear gunner said he had blacked out temporarily.

Two more aircraft were seen on Fishpond, but not by the gunners at 2333 hrs and 2335 hrs, and evasive action was taken and both enemy aircraft were lost. Again at 2344 hrs an aircraft was picked up on Fishpond. It was then seen by both gunners (who gave evasive action) for fleeting glimpses in cloud. This aircraft was unidentified.

At 2350 hrs 4000' – picked up on Fishpond. Me410 picked up by rear gunner who gave evasive action. He attempted to open fire but found all guns u/s. Picked up by Mid upper. Owing to being so near the ground most unorthodox evasive action was taken. Enemy aircraft next came in from starboard quarter up 300 yards away. Mid upper gave him a long burst. He crossed over to port quarter. Mid upper gave him another long burst. His port motor and port wing burst into flames and he dived steeply into low cloud. Aircraft OF–H also went into cloud at this moment and no further result was seen. The ground was only 600 to 800' below and this fact is considered reasonable grounds to believe that the enemy aircraft was unlikely to reach its base and was probably destroyed. In all between 2321 hrs and 2350 hrs aircraft OF-H was attacked 9 times.

The Mid Upper Gunner, F/L Jones fired 1,500 rounds and the Rear Gunner, F/Sgt Noall, fired 4,500 rounds in this unique encounter. Not many aircraft claimed three enemy fighters destroyed in their whole career, never mind in *one* night. F/L Albert Henry Jones had already been awarded the DFC on 22-8-44 and Flt Sgt William Dennis Noall was to be awarded the DFM two weeks after the Karlsruhe raid, his award being promulgated in the London Gazette on 16-2-45. On the same night, F/O Watson's 97 Sqn Lancaster had just dropped its last flare when they were attacked by a Ju88 making two determined attacks on the aircraft. P/O Watson corkscrewed away and his Mid-Upper, Flt Sgt Milford drove the attacker off.

144

With regards to the award of decorations, a sobering fact is that the Distinguished Flying Cross was awarded more often than the Distinguished Flying Medal. Given the fact that there were more NCO aircrew than officer aircrew it may come as a shock to realise that DFC's were awarded on a scale of five to one when compared to the DFM and that Wireless Operator's hardly featured in awards of the latter.

There is no doubt at all that Leslie's calm and professional manner in the use of Fishpond to warn his crew of the presence of fighters bearing down on them greatly assisted in the destruction of the enemy nightfighters and contributed to OF-H's safe arrival back at Coningsby. A modest man, he would demur if pressed but had it not been for his timely interventions the aircraft and crew could quite well have been lost that night.

Karlsruhe: 250 Lancasters and 11 Mosquitoes of No 5 Group. 14 Lancasters lost. No 189 Squadron, from Fulbeck, lost 4 of its 19 aircraft on the raid. Cloud cover over the target caused this raid to be a complete failure. Karlsruhe reports no casualties and only a few bombs. The report mentions 'dive bombers', presumably the Mosquito marker aircraft trying to establish their position. This was a lucky escape for Karlsruhe in its last major RAF raid of the war.

On the night of 7/8th February, a 97 Sqn Lancaster OF-N, registration ND961 and flown by Lt C.W.McGregor SAAF collided over the town of Best (Nord-Brabant.) in Holland with another Lancaster from 83 Sqn on a raid to the Dortmund-Ems Canal at Ladbergen. All onboard OF-N were killed, including the Visual Air Bomber, F/L G.S.Johnston DFC and Bar. From the other aircraft, OL-C, registration PB181 and flown by F/Sgt G. Summers, there was just one survivor, F/L A.P. Weber who was thrown

145

clear and descended by parachute. All the dead were recovered and buried in Holland.

On the 10th operations were cancelled owing to poor weather forecast on the return leg but as the aircrafts bomb-loads were being removed a 1000lb bomb fell off an 83 Sqn trolley at Coningsby and exploded, killing two ground crew and damaging several of the parked Lancasters.

On the 13/14th February, 11 aircraft from 97 Sqn took off to participate in what has since become one of the most controversial raids of the war, 'Operation Thunderclap' the bombing of Dresden. Stalin had long been pressing Churchill for assistance in attacking vital communication and railway centres behind the Eastern Front as the Russians ploughed their way into Eastern Germany.

Churchill and his staff agreed and a series of targets were worked out. Dresden featured high on the list, along with Chemnitz and Leipzig. Dresden was also known to be packed with German refugees and wounded and it was thought that a morale-breaking raid on the city would finish any German enthusiasm to continue the war effort.

The raid was split into two phases. The first wave would consist entirely of 5 Group aircraft and accordingly, the 11 Lancasters from 97 Sqn, together with other marker aircraft from 83 Squadron and 9 Mosquitoes marked the target as a force of 244 Lancasters dropped 800 tons of bombs and incendiaries on the city. Cloud in the target area meant the first attack was only moderately successful and all the 97 Sqn aircraft returned safely. Harry Brooker's crew had been stood down from this operation and did not participate.

Three hours later, as the city was recovering, another all Lancaster force of 529 Lancasters swept across the beleaguered city dropping more than 1,800 tons of bombs and incendiaries with great accuracy. A firestorm similar to that experienced in the Hamburg raids of 1943 ensued and the casualty rate was horrific. To make matters worse, 311 B-17 Flying Fortresses of the American 8th Air Force dropped 771 tons on the city the following day, stoking the fires raging in the city and adding to the casualty lists. The raids cost the RAF 6 Lancasters over the target, with 2 more crashing in France on the way home and 1 aircraft crashing in England. It is thought that over 40,000 people lost their lives in Dresden that night and some historians have indicated that the figures may be over 50,000. Postwar, in a disgraceful act of betrayal, Churchill distanced himself from the bombing leaving the bemused survivors of Bomber Command alone to suffer the opprobrium and accusations of murderers being heaped on their shoulders.

83 Sqn would face another tragedy on the 22nd February when the Coningsby Station Commander, Gp Capt A.C. Evans Evans DFC, flying OL-Y was shot down over Holland by a Ju88 nightfighter with only the rear gunner W/O Hansen DFC surviving. At 43, Gp Capt Evans Evans was one of the oldest senior officers killed on flying operations during the entire war. In stark contrast his navigator that night, Squadron Leader 'Jock' Wishart DSO DFC and Bar, was only 22; the youngest Sqn Leader to be killed on operations.

On the same operation, the 97 Sqn aircraft of F/O Warnock was attacked by two Ju88's and only a spirited defence of the aircraft by the two gunners, W/O Channon DFM in the mid-upper position and F/Sgt Wilkins in the rear turret, drove off their determined attackers.

The following night, the 23rd February, ten 97 Sqn crews were among the 83 Lancasters and Mosquitoes of 5 Group which attacked the U-boat base and shipping in the port of Horten in Oslo Fiord, Norway. Only one aircraft was lost, a 97 Sqn aircraft OF-E, registration PB588, flown by F/O B.J.Hines. During a fierce fight with a Ju88, the aircraft was seen to catch fire and although other aircraft reported seeing parachutes deployed from the stricken aircraft, all the crew were killed. The rear-gunner, F/L John Ray, a married man from Chippenham was 38 years old, well above the average age for a bomber crew member. OF-E was an aircraft Leslie and the crew had previously flown in on the Heilbronn raid of 4/5th December.

During these fraught operations, Leslie and his fellow crew members were enjoying a well-earned break from operations, having been awarded two weeks leave and a further two weeks rest from operations until the time came for them to board a Lancaster once more. On this occasion, it was to a target the squadron had visited more than once before, the heavily-defended Dortmund-Ems canal. Poor weather had seen the cancellation of a proposed daylight raid on the canal on the 28th February and it was re-scheduled for the night of the 3rd/4th March.

31.   3/4th March 1945 – Ladbergen. (Dortmund-Ems Canal.)

OF-K. PB905. F/L H.Brooker, Sgt W.J.Morgan, F/L K.Brown, F/Sgt D.J.Hector, **F/Sgt L.B.Smith**, F/L A.H.Jones, F/Sgt A. D'Arcy. Up 1837 Down 2345. Bomb load 14 CP No1. 10/10ths cloud, thin layer, approx 5000ft. Identified target on H2S. Glow of green TI's seen through cloud. Flares dropped as briefed. Controller found target immediately and Green TI was assessed as accurate.

212 Lancasters and 10 Mosquitoes of No 5 Group attacked the Ladbergen aqueduct on the Dortmund-Ems Canal, breached it in 2 places and put it completely out of action. 7 Lancasters lost. The gunners in the No 619 Squadron Lancaster of Wing Commander SG Birch claimed to have shot down a V-1 flying bomb near the target area; the V-1 was probably aimed at the port of Antwerp.

The Luftwaffe mounted Operation Gisella on this night, sending approximately 200 night fighters to follow the various bomber forces to England. This move took the British defences partly by surprise and the Germans shot down 20 bombers - 8 Halifaxes of No 4 Group, 2 Lancasters of No 5 Group, 3 Halifaxes, 1 Fortress and 1 Mosquito of No 100 Group and 3 Lancasters and 2 Halifaxes from the Heavy Conversion Units which had been taking part in the diversionary sweep. 3 of the German fighters crashed, through flying too low; the German fighter which crashed near Elvington airfield was the last Luftwaffe aircraft to crash on English soil during the war.

32. 5/6th March 1945 – Bohlen.

OF-K. PB905. F/L H.Brooker, Sgt W.J.Morgan, S/L T.Campbell, F/Sgt D.J.Hector, **F/Sgt L.B.Smith,** F/L A.H.Jones, F/Sgt A.D'Arcy. Up 1659 Down 0252. Bomb load 12 CP No 1, 2 x Wanganui flares G/R. 10/10ths cloud, tops 10/11000ft. Target located on H2S. Dropped flares as briefed. Received Controller's orders for sky marking at 21.43hrs. Orbited but could not identify target sufficiently well again to drop Wanganui's. Large flash of an explosion lasting about 3 secs at 2152hrs approx. Green TI seen to drop at 2129 hrs and appeared to be to the west of the target.

248 Lancasters and 10 Mosquitoes of No 5 Group attacked the synthetic-oil refinery at Böhlen. The target area was covered by cloud but some damage was caused to the refinery. 4 Lancasters lost.

14 crews from 97 Sqn were part of the force that attacked Bohlen. Because of the thick cloud obscuring the

target, 'Wanganui' sky-marking flares in Green and Red colours were used to very good effect. A photographic reconnaissance mission to Bohlen two days later confirmed that the plant was now out of action. Leslie's crew were one of the last to return from a tiring 8hr flight in cloud all the way out and back. They were stood down from the following night's raid to Sassnitz, near Stettin, East Germany.

'Although by this time of the war we were continually being briefed that the German nightfighter force was beaten, the flak hadn't diminished at all. During the approach and run-in to the target I was too busy to notice much other than the flashes outside my window and a noise like hail as bits of shrapnel hit the airframe. It was only back at the debrief that the rest of the crew would tell me how intense the flak had been that night. Maybe that was a good thing as it meant I had less to worry about!'

33. 7/8th March 1945 – Harburg.
OF-K. PB905. F/L H.Brooker, Sgt W.J.Morgan, F/L K.Brown, F/Sgt D.J.Hector, **F/Sgt L.B.Smith**, F/L A.H.Jones, F/Sgt A.D'Arcy. Up 1809 Down 0008. Bomb load 12 CP No 12 RP Flares G/R. About 5/10ths thin cloud at 13,000ft. Target located on H2S. We had a very good run with no trouble at all and the dropping was satisfactory. Two Green TI seen in dock area and one about one mile or two south. Flares in general were excellent. Red markers were clearly seen. Bombing was observed on leaving target. Two or three explosions, especially a large one at approx 22.10hrs. Fires and a pall of smoke up to 9/10,000ft by 22.15 hrs.

234 Lancasters and 7 Mosquitoes of No 5 Group carried out an accurate attack on the oil refinery at Harburg. 14 Lancasters lost. No 189 Squadron, from Fulbeck, lost 4 of its 16 Lancasters on the raid. One local report states that a rubber factory was seriously damaged as well as the oil targets.

15 crews from 97 Sqn took part in the raid against Harburg, south of Hamburg. All returned safely although fierce flak over the target caused damage to two aircraft. Despite fourteen 5 Group aircraft being lost on the raid, no fighter opposition was encountered by any of the 97 Sqn aircraft.

'On the 12th March 1945, I discovered that I'd been promoted to Acting Warrant Officer (Paid.) another step-up in rank, pay and privileges. It meant being able to wear officer-type clothing made of Barethea cloth, an overt display of the step up in status. A further privilege granted in May 1945 was the permanent award of the Pathfinder Badge. The authorities deemed that the need to complete 45 operations had been curtailed by the end of hostilities and this was confirmed by a certificate entitling me to wear the badge on a permanent basis'

34. 14/15th March 1945 – Lützkendorf.
OF-K. PB905. F/L H.Brooker, Sgt W.J.Morgan, F/L K.Brown, F/Sgt D.J.Hector, **F/Sgt L.B.Smith**, F/L A.H.Jones, F/Sgt A.D'Arcy. Up 1658 Down 0158. Bomb load 4 x 1000lb MC (delay), 2 x 1000lb TI Green, 2 x Wanganui flares G/R. Cloud; hazy below. Target located on H2S. No illumination down when we arrived. On run up, one load of Green TI's seen to cascade. Made orbit, and three green TI's seen forming a line from west to east,

approx 3/400 yards long. Diverted to and landed at Wing.

244 Lancasters and 11 Mosquitoes of No 5 Group attacked the Wintershall synthetic-oil refinery at Lützkendorf. Photographic reconnaissance showed that 'moderate damage' was caused. 18 Lancasters were lost, 7.4 per cent of the Lancaster force.

18 crews endured the 9½hrs return flight to Lützkendorf in poor visibility and thick cloud. Owing to the weather the raid was unsuccessful and on returning to Lincolnshire, all the squadron aircraft diverted to other airfields due to fog, many with fuel tanks almost empty.

35. 16/17 March 1945 - Würzburg

OF-E. PB133. F/L H.Brooker, Sgt W.J.Morgan, F/L K.Brown, F/Sgt D.J.Hector, **F/Sgt L.B.Smith**, F/L A.H.Jones, F/Sgt A.D'Arcy. Up 1734 Down 0109. 12 CP No 1 2 x 250lb TI Green. No cloud; clear. Target located on green TI. At least three green TI's were seen in town, with apparently one on the H2S M/P. Illumination good. Concentration of reds seen. After leaving target bombing appeared well concentrated. 2 x 250lb TI's not required.

225 Lancasters and 11 Mosquitoes of No 5 Group attacked Würzburg. 6 Lancasters lost. This was another dramatic and devastating blow by No 5 Group. 1,127 tons of bombs were dropped with great accuracy in 17 minutes. According to a post-war survey, the old cathedral city with its famous historic buildings suffered 89 per cent of its built-up area destroyed. Würzburg contained little industry and this was an area attack.

'We were one of thirteen 97 Sqn aircraft despatched that night and on leaving the target area over

Würzburg, I picked up several fast-moving blips on the Fishpond screen closing at a high speed and travelling faster than any German fighter we'd been briefed on. Evasive action was swiftly taken by Harry Brooker and the aircraft overshot leaving both fighters and bomber to carry on their respective ways. At the debrief after landing safely we were informed that the aircraft were German jet fighters, the Messerschmitt Me262 operating in the nightfighter role.'

The first kill at night for the Me262 occurred in December 1944 but it was used mainly against Mosquitoes, Oberleutnant Kurt Welter of JG300 whose total of 56 victories included several against these aircraft in 1945 being one of the more successful pilots.

Their CO, Group Captain Johnson, had grave doubts about the choice of target that night and had telephoned HQ to query the reasoning behind the operation. He was told that the operation would go and after reflecting on whether to refuse to accompany the force decided to participate at the last moment, albeit with grave misgivings. Nuremburg was also being attacked that night by 8 Group, the two operations being planned to merge at the same time to split the nightfighter strength. The 5 Group attack on Würzburg was slightly ahead of schedule and as they banked away, Leslie could see the orange glow from Nuremberg lighting up the sky. The nightfighters homed in on the glare and 8 Group lost 24 Lancasters, Leslie witnessed some of the mid-air explosions of the stricken aircraft from his position in the astrodome but it was not until the following morning that they heard just how grievous the losses had been.

The grim cost of operational flying was further brought home to Leslie during March when on successive nights,

97 Squadron lost an aircraft, both of which the Brooker crew had flown in on raids during December 1944. (OF-Q on 17/18th December and OF-A on 19/20th and 21/22nd December.)

Lancaster OF-A, registration PA973 and flown by F/O J.D. Cottman RAAF was lost without trace on the night of 20/21st March on a raid to Bohlen. This was an all-Australian crew. All were known and mourned by Leslie and his fellow NCO's.

The following night, 21/22nd March, another 97 Sqn Lancaster was lost with OF-Q, registration PB521 and piloted by F/L O.P.Taylor DFC RNZAF falling victim to flak on a raid to Hamburg. The aircraft crashed in flames near Feldmark Leesig. Three of the crew bailed out, the others dying in the aircraft but the rear gunner F/Sgt W.T. Bray was reported to have fallen into the nearby River Este and drowned after successfully landing on *terra firma*.

Other reports from Italian prisoners-of-war who witnessed F/Sgt Bray's descent say he was murdered by German civilians after landing by parachute, being struck over the head and then pushed into the river to drown. W/O J.H. Bushby survived to become a POW and although the pilot, F/L Taylor, bailed out successfully, he succumbed to his severe injuries and died in a POW camp a month later. OF-Q was the last aircraft lost by 97 Sqn during WW2.

F/L Charles Eaton DFC and Bar and his crew completed their 97 Sqn Pathfinder tour of 45 operations in spectacular fashion on the Hamburg raid. Hit by heavy flak at 18,000ft their aircraft plunged 15,000ft before Eaton regained control of the aircraft. Flying low over the target at only 3,000ft and being fired at by every anti-aircraft gun, or so it seemed, Eaton brought his damaged Lancaster back to Coningsby on three engines for a well-earned two weeks leave and a stand-down from operational flying.

36. 8/9th April 1945.Lützkendorf.

OF-K. PB905. F/L H.Brooker, Sgt W.J.Morgan, F/L K.Brown, F/Sgt D.J.Hector, **F/Sgt L.B.Smith**, F/L A.H.Jones, F/Sgt A.D'Arcy. Up 1804 Down 0233. Bomb load 12 CP No 1, 2 x Wanganui flares G/R. Clear; target identified on H2S, with visual check. There were two green TI's about 600/800 yds apart. Illumination seemed concentrated. After leaving target, bombing appeared concentrated. At 22.53 there was a big explosion followed by another at 2301. Our Wanganui flares not required. H2S was intermittent, and as green TI's were down, we dropped visually on the greens with a box check. Landed at Lichfield.

231 Lancasters and 11 Mosquitoes of No 5 Group attacked the Lützkendorf oil refinery, which had escaped serious damage the previous night. The refinery was rendered 'inactive'. 6 Lancasters lost.

97 Sqn were given a welcome break from operations after the Hamburg raid for the next few weeks, concentrating on flying training instead. Operations resumed on the 7/8th April when 14 crews attacked a Benzol plant at Molbis near Leipzig. For another lucky crew, that of Squadron Leader Richard Canever DFC, Leipzig was their 55th and final operation. The next night 15 crews were despatched to Lützkendorf, another long flight to a target the Brooker crew had encountered previously. Clear weather saw accurate flak but the bombing put the plant out of action, and fog on their return to Coningsby saw Leslie's crew divert yet again, this time to RAF Lichfield.

On the 10/11th April, 5 crews from 97 Sqn attacked the Wahren railway yards in Leipzig without loss. Poor weather grounded the Lancasters until 16/17th April when

13 crews attacked the railway yards at Pilsen. Leslie's crew was stood down from both of these operations, crews being rotated as the war drew to a close and the need for large numbers of Pathfinders over the targets abated. Their penultimate operation was carried out the following night when they joined 11 crews from 97 Sqn who took off to illuminate the railway marshalling yards in Cham.

37. 17/18th April 1945 – Cham.

OF-K. PB905. F/L H.Brooker, Sgt W.J.Morgan, F/L K.Brown, F/Sgt D.J.Hector, **F/Sgt L.B.Smith**, F/L A.H.Jones, F/Sgt A.D'Arcy. Up 2342 Down 0726. Bomb load 14 CP No 1. Clear, moderate visibility over target, located on H2S confirming GPS run. Two green TI's seen, and they appeared accurate. Flares appeared to drop short, but gave adequate illumination. Red TI's seen to fall and were assessed by Controller and Marker Leader as accurate.

90 Lancasters and 11 Mosquitoes of No 5 Group attacked the railway yards in the small town of Cham deep in south-eastern Germany. The attack was completely successful, with tracks torn up and rolling stock destroyed. No aircraft lost.

97 Squadron's penultimate operation was carried out on the night of 18/19th April when 11 aircraft attacked the railway yards at Komotau in Czechoslovakia. The bombing was a complete success and all crews returned safely. For Leslie and his comrades the end was in sight but before they could celebrate they joined with the force of 11 Lancasters from 97 Sqn who carried out the squadron's last operation when they illuminated the oil refinery at Tonsberg in southern Norway. Sqn Leader Taylor's aircraft was the last to return safely to Coningsby,

landing at 2.53am and bringing 97 Squadron's part in the war to an end.

38. 25/26th April 1945 – Tonsberg.

OF-K. PB905. F/L H.Brooker, Sgt W.J.Morgan, F/L K.Brown, F/Sgt D.J.Hector, **W/O L.B.Smith**, F/O J.L.Barton, F/Sgt A.D'Arcy. Up 2045 Down 0236. 14 CP No 1. 9/10ths cloud, tops about 9000ft. Target identified on H2S. Controller was unable to contact Link 1, so asked for any link. We (Link 3) answered and received no reply from him; then Link 4 called up, and Controller told him to carry on. Through cloud green TI appeared to be in good position. Flares appeared to be well concentrated. Rear gunner reported explosion in target area at 23.48.5 hrs.

107 Lancasters and 12 Mosquitoes of No 5 Group attacked the oil refinery in Tonsberg in Southern Norway in the last raid flown by heavy bombers. The attack was accurately carried out and the target was severely damaged. A Lancaster of No 463 Squadron came down in Sweden, the last of more than 3,300 Lancasters lost in the war; Flying Officer A Cox and his all-British crew all survived and were interned in Sweden until the end of the war - only a few days away.

The Tonsberg raid was the last operation Harry Brooker, Leslie and the crew participated in. Since July 1944 they had flown on 38 operations, ranging from short daylight operations against flying bomb sites in the Pas de Calais to 10 hour flights at night deep into the heart of the German Reich. They had accomplished what over 55,000 of their fellow Bomber Command aircrew had failed to do, survive the air war over Occupied Europe.

By a remarkable coincidence, OF-K was accompanied to Tonsberg by ten Lancasters of 61 Squadron, Leslie and the Brooker crew ending their tour of operations alongside aircraft from the very squadron with whom they'd started their operational flying.

97 Squadron PFF lost 123 aircraft during the war and carried out a total of 4,091 sorties over some of the most heavily defended targets in Occupied Europe, leaving the graves of over 750 of its aircrew scattered throughout the countryside's of France, Belgium, Denmark, Holland, Norway and Germany. Included in that number are those squadron aircrew whose bodies were recovered on British soil and buried in Britain. A few, the lucky few, survived their airborne experiences and landed to become prisoners of war in the many POW camps scattered throughout Europe.

On the 30th April 1945, Adolf Hitler and his new bride, Eva Braun, committed suicide within the bunker deep beneath the Reichs Chancellory in embattled Berlin. Four days later, representatives of the German armed forces met with their allied counterparts with a view to a conditional surrender but this was flatly rejected and the Germans signed an unconditional surrender on the 7th May on Lüneberg Heath in Northern Germany. Victory was signalled by VE Day, 'Victory in Europe' on the 8th May and caused quiet satisfaction to Leslie and all the airmen at Coningsby, the elation not surfacing fully until a week later when several raucous parties took place.

The victory had come at a cost. In the eleven months of savage fighting since D-Day in June 1944 the British Army lost 40,000 men. By comparison, in the same period Bomber Command lost 2,128 aircraft with over 10,000 aircrew killed. From January 1st 1945, although Germany's ability to defend herself in the air was severely diminished, Bomber Command's losses were 711 aircraft, over 5,600 men killed or POW's.

The 2/3rd of May 1945 holds a poignant memory in the history of WW2, being the last date on which RAF aircrew were killed on operations. On that date a Mosquito of 169 Squadron was lost whilst carrying out a low-level napalm attack on Jagel airfield near Kiel. Both crew members were killed. On the same night two Halifax's of 199 Squadron forming part of the radar-suppressing *'Mandrel'* screen collided in the Weimersdorf area near Kiel with only three men from the two aircraft surviving.

During the six years of the war, Bomber Command carried out 392,137 sorties, dropping over 955,000 tons of bombs. Amongst the many medals awarded to her members were 19 Victoria Crosses, many of them posthumous. Bomber Command's losses on operations during that period were a total of 8,325 aircraft with 72% of aircrew lost being British, 18% Canadian, 7% Australian and 3% New Zealanders.

For all those souls lost and whose remains were never recovered, their names were recorded for posterity on the RAF memorial at Runnymede overlooking the meadow adjoining the River Thames where Magna Carta was signed. It is fitting that they be remembered in sight of the field wherein the great document enshrining the common man's basic freedom under law was signed. Engraved on the Great North Window of the shrine are the moving words of the 139th Psalm, sometimes known as 'The Airman's Psalm'.

If I climb up into Heaven, Though art there;
If I go to Hell, Thou art there also.
If I take the wings of the morning
And remain in the uttermost parts of the sea,
Even there also shall Thy hand lead me;
And Thy right hand shall hold me.

The last Lancaster to be lost by 97 Squadron came two days after Germany's surrender, when, on the 10th May, OF-Z, registration ME623 and flown by F/L Arnott crashed on take-off from Evere airfield near Brussels. She was bringing freed British POW's back to Britain as part of 'Operation Exodus' when she crashed and caught fire. No serious injuries were reported but the aircraft was a write-off.

The squadron had already been placed on high alert to repatriate many of the incarcerated POW's in many camps in Germany and so any celebrations had been put on hold. During the next few weeks, as well as flights to return the POW's to Britain, the squadron also undertook daylight flights over Germany in order to show the many ground crew members the results of their long, tiring hours keeping the aircraft serviceable in all weathers. Many were visibly shocked to see the utter devastation area bombing had had on the cities of Germany where whole districts were empty, burnt-out shells with few walls still standing.

Group Captain Johnson, CO of 97 Squadron, in his thoughtful memoirs 'Withered Garland' published after the war quoted JB Priestley's thought on bombing. Priestley wrote:

'The fact remains that this indiscriminate mass bombing is a terrible and obscene business. It belongs to the nightmare side of things. It is like some old, ugly dream come true. It cuts deeper, as I know from my own experience, than fighting at the front. And, for this reason, that it is warfare at its foulest, all mixed up with women and children, with familiar surroundings, with houses and shops, libraries and hospitals.'

It is doubtful that Leslie Smith and his comrades who were involved in the campaign, together with the many thousands of their fellow crewmembers who gave their lives in that campaign, would agree with him. War in itself is an ugly, foul and obscene business and arguments still reign today on the rights and wrongs of the Allies conduct of the war. Many of those who vilify the night-time area bombing of Germany during World War Two have the luxury of hindsight and ignore the fact that bombing accuracy was still in its infancy, even with the later more accurate methods such as OBOE.

To mitigate the mounting losses of a daylight campaign the RAF had switched to night bombing which undoubtedly saved many British and Commonwealth aircrew lives, the war needed to be won and at the time this was the only weapon available to take the fight to Germany and her allies. To pour hatred and scorn on the shoulders of those tasked with carrying out this task dishonours the memory of those who fought and unhesitatingly died for their ideals, something sadly lacking in the modern world.

Meanwhile, for 97 Squadron, the end of the war brought no end to their flying operations with H2S training flights, Cross-country flights and a fresh Fighter Affiliation programme prior to the advent of 'Operation Exodus'. Even before the formal surrender was signed, squadron Lancasters began flying missions to Germany and formerly Occupied Europe to begin the heartening task of flying the many thousands of Prisoner of War personnel, all eager to return to Britain and their families. Six 97 Sqn aircraft flew on 4th May, seven on the 7th, five on the 8th, 12 on the 9th, followed by 16 on the 10th and another 12 on the 11th. The Brooker crew's turn came on the 9th May.

'On the 9th May, our crew took part in 'Operation Exodus', flying to Rheine in Germany to repatriate some of the many thousands of ex-POW's. I can still remember the gratitude of these men who had suffered many years as prisoners of the Germans and how they were overjoyed to be given sweets, chocolates and cigarettes for the flight back to Britain.'

97 Squadron's Operational Log for May 1945 shows the following strength in aircrew and sorties which includes all the mercy flights they carried out:

Total Strength: Officers—112. NCO's—138.
Total Operational Hours for Month: 70hrs 5mins.
Total Non-operational Hours for Month: 596hrs 45 mins.
Total Sorties for Month: Nil.
Total Sorties since Formation: 4,091.

So ended the war for this fine squadron.

Recriminations would come later and with them the accusations of being murderers, given that estimates of German civilian deaths during the war due to the bombing campaign alone were over 400,000. The RAF dropped over 955,000 *tons* of bombs on Germany over six years of war and there is no doubt that the sacrifices of so many of Bomber Command's finest hastened the wars end. In countering the bomber assault, Germany was forced to divert thousands of guns for anti-aircraft defence that could have been used in the land battles and retain over 1,000,000 troops in Germany to man those defences, men that were sorely needed on the front-line.

The RAF aircrew survivors would become caught up in a political campaign that virtually disowned them, Arthur Harris and Don Bennett were both left out of any meaningful Honours Lists after the war and Harris retired in disgust to South Africa when his pleas for a specific campaign medal for Bomber Command were rejected out of hand.

American 8th Air Force aircrew were presented with an Air Medal for every five missions they completed and on completion of the twenty-five missions that constituted a tour were awarded a Distinguished Flying Cross and returned home to the USA, their war service complete.

Some American aircrew saw out their stressful and dangerous war service in a matter of only two months, flying their twenty-five missions in a fairly short space of time and taking no further part in the war.

For Bomber Command there was no special medal to commemorate their sacrifice. After D-Day the Aircrew Europe Star was discontinued and aircrew were simply awarded the France and Germany Star, the same medal as worn by rear echelon servicemen on the ground who never came within a hundred miles of the fighting. Thus did Britain tardily reward her fighting men who nightly and almost single-handedly took the war to Germany for over four dark years whilst losing half their numbers in the process.

Leslie's contribution to the war effort and his reward for thirty-eight fraught operations over Occupied Europe was the award of the 1939-45 Star, France and Germany Star, Defence and War Medal, along with the freedom to permanently wear the Pathfinder badge with his medals.

One happy bit of news concerning medals was the award of a Distinguished Flying Cross to their navigator. F/L Kennedy Brown's DFC was promulgated on 21-9-45 and recognised the sterling work he had carried out in navigating them to and from the target under arduous conditions. 'Ken' Brown had also been lent out on several occasions to the Oboe-equipped Mosquitoes of the Pathfinder Force when they requested his services, having earlier recognised his abilities with the Brooker crew.

Shortly after Germany's surrender, Leslie had word that he was to be transferred to 'Tiger Force', a Group equipping with the newly-introduced Avro Lincoln, successor to the Lancaster and destined for the Far East. Although VE Day, (Victory in Europe) had come and gone, the Japanese were still fighting fiercely against the United States forces and it was decided that a force of British

163

bombers would be sent to aid them in their efforts. After being posted to Banbury, Oxfordshire, to await further orders, the dropping of two atomic bombs on Hiroshima and Nagasaki heralded Japan's surrender and the end of the war on August 15th. With Japan's surrender Leslie's war also came to a welcome end.

Fifty-five years after the war, in 2001 Leslie received a telephone call from Harry Brooker's widow, Marge, who was ringing to ask if he had any information about a former RNZAF bomber aircrewman, Jim Pearce. Jim's sister had rung Marge from New Zealand to ascertain the truth of a story Jim had told his family after the war and Leslie was happy to confirm the veracity of the tale:

'Whilst serving with 97 Squadron we were on our way back from a bombing mission when we caught up with a fellow Lancaster on the French side of the English Channel, smoke pouring from one of its engines. Our instructions were to leave any such aircraft to make its own way back but knowing such stragglers were easy targets, Harry Brooker deliberately throttled back and slowly formated on the stricken aircraft, escorting it all the way back to Coningsby under the protection of our own aircraft's guns.'

F/O James Pearce DFC flew as the eighth member of Leslie's crew for thirteen operations between November 1944 and February 1945. Some Pathfinder Lancasters carried an eighth crewman with them as a Visual Bomb Aimer, complementing the usual bomb aimer who now operated the H2S set and Jim Pearce never forgot Harry Brooker's bravery that day. As well as keeping the crew of the aircraft safe, Harry's actions meant a valuable aircraft could fly again after its damage was repaired. As Leslie recalled,

'**Whilst we might not have agreed with his actions, we were all too aware of the gratitude of the other aircraft's crew in regarding Harry Brooker's outstanding bravery that day.**'

Epilogue

Although the war had ended, Leslie's flying career carried on with an overseas posting to Transport Command and in June 1945 he travelled to Bramcote, near Nuneaton, to join 105 OTU. This was an Operational Training Unit engaged in training crews on the DC-3 Douglas Dakota cargo aircraft. Shortly after his arrival the unit disbanded but reformed as 1381 Transport Conversion Unit and Leslie's training along with fellow members of the unit continued unabated.

He soon found himself on a ferry flight to India with stopovers in Malta and Tripoli, where he was briefly hospitalised by a septic insect bite. Fully fit, he travelled on to what is now Karachi in Pakistan before being based between Maripur and Baroda in India. Baroda lies in the state of Gujarat and was an important town on the main road between Delhi and Bombay. For the next few months Leslie and his fellow aircrew flew supply missions all over India in their Dakotas, delivering VIP's, troops and cargo to the various garrison towns and cities.

After two hundred years in India, British rule was coming to an end with Independence and Partition looming so after only a few months enjoying the heat but not the monsoon storms that drenched them on a daily basis, Leslie's sojourn overseas came to an end. Posted back to Catterick, in May 1946 Warrant Officer Leslie Bruce Smith found himself a civilian. It was not to be the end of his contact with the RAF as Leslie would re-enlist, briefly, in 1956 when the Suez crisis erupted and his logbook shows the many flights he took after the war as a crewman in Ansons in a Reserve role. For now, though, the 24yr old ex-Pathfinder wireless operator found himself back in civilian life seeking a different kind of employment.

Returning to Aberdeen, Leslie resumed his employment with the Northern Co-op at Berryden Road but within a year knew it was not for him. Flying had fostered a deep yearning for adventure and it wasn't long before another opportunity arose. A chance meeting with an old friend, Graham Robertson, who'd served on Air Sea rescue launches during the war provided what seemed to be the chance of a lifetime. Graham had obtained his Bosun's ticket as a result of his service and was on his way down to Lowestoft to join an expedition that promised a great deal to anyone at a crossroads in their life. Leslie wryly remarked, **'Graham didn't so much ask me to join him, he demanded I did!'**

In May 1925, the famous explorer Colonel Percival Harrison Fawcett together with his oldest son Jack and another companion, Raleigh Rimell, mounted an expedition in the Matto Grosso region of Brazil to find what he believed to be a lost Inca city full of gold and other precious objects. Nothing was heard of them after they set off from the Brazilian city of Cuiaba and for many years afterwards rumours persisted that he was still alive and living in the hinterland.

Over the next decades, many expeditions set out to find Colonel Fawcett, none of them successful in finding either the missing explorer or the fabled lost city. Graham Robertson was on his way to England to join with a group of men determined to journey to the Matto Grosso and find the truth and the Colonel if he was still alive. The tale appealed to Leslie's sense of adventure and he joined up with the expedition led an ex-RAF officer, Sqn Leader Falgate and crewed by an experienced skipper, Claud R Spriggs of Leicester..

Together the six men each contributed £600, a large sum in those days, to buy and outfit an ex-Lowestoft herring drifter named the *Present Friend*. The object of the expedition was to steam across the Atlantic and enter the

Amazon river. After making their way upstream to Fawcett's last-known whereabouts the expedition would then attempt to find him and his companions using all the information at hand.

With all their worldly belongings stowed on the ship they set off with high hopes, hugging the coastline towards Cornwall before striking out into the Atlantic. Nearing the Lizard disaster struck when the ship's pumps failed and they began to take in large volumes of water. Sinking ever lower in the water a distress call was transmitted and the ship was towed into the comparative safety of Helford sound near Falmouth. The following morning the tide rose but the ship didn't, completely waterlogged she sank at her moorings. She took with her not only their hopes of adventure but most of Leslie's memorabilia, diaries, his aircrew logbook and all the notes he'd kept prior to setting off. As he watched his life, literally, drift out to sea on the tide Leslie decided it was time he returned to Scotland and settle for a more mundane life.

Back in the Granite City Leslie found a series of labouring jobs, one of which entailed unloading ships laden with lime destined for fertiliser. Becoming friends with the foreman, he was taken on as a trade rep for the Aberdeen Lime Co and began a more settled life of employment. That opportunity led to a meeting in 1951 and employment with Steel Coulson Beers, a brewery based in Edinburgh but whose roots were the North-east of England. It was a two-year deal with salary, expenses but no company car and a defined territory to explore and improve sales.

Whilst working for them Leslie agreed to make up a foursome with some friends who were going to the *Palais de Danse* ballroom in Diamond Street, Aberdeen. The lovely young woman, Elizabeth Hutcheon, who was to be his partner caught his eye and they began to see each other on a more frequent basis, a courtship which led to their marriage in 1951.

Leslie threw himself into his work and before long was head-hunted as a rep by the brewers, James Aitken Ltd of Falkirk. Unfortunately, his new boss and Leslie didn't see eye to eye with each other and Leslie was soon on his way to a far more happier arrangement with William McEwans, a brewing company that later grew into Scottish and Newcastle. Leslie was to spend the next thirty two years with the company, rising to the position of Area Sales Manager and bringing to the position the same qualities and commitment he had espoused in his service life.

During that time his marriage to 'Bess', as she was known, had blessed the couple with four children, Alison, Helen, Leslie and Elizabeth. Moving from Aberdeen to Dyce, the family finally settled in Inverurie, where Bess took over the reins at the Golf Shop at Inverurie Golf Club. It was there that Leslie joined her after taking voluntary redundancy from Scottish and Newcastle and the couple enjoyed a harmonious working life for the next five years before selling the business to begin a well-earned retirement together.

In their time in Dyce and Inverurie Leslie entered local politics, ending as a Councillor on both Dyce and Inverurie Town Councils where he served for nearly forty years altogether. A prized letter addressed to him personally from Alex Salmond, Scotland's First Minister, praised those achievements on his retirement when he finally stepped down. A past President, at 89yrs of age Leslie still finds time to attend the Inverurie Probus Club every fortnight and listen keenly to the guest speakers.

His flying career had almost faded into the distant past when a friend popped in to see him. Stanley Johnstone had travelled down to a Toastmaster's Convention in England and whilst there had struck up a conversation with a fellow delegate who'd been a bomber pilot during the war. When Stanley informed the man about his friend in Aberdeen who'd been a wireless operator on Lancasters during the war, he was thunderstruck to find that his fellow delegate was Harry Brooker, Leslie's old pilot and crewmember.

Pilot and wireless operator were soon back in touch with each other after a gap of twenty years and Harry and Marge travelled to Aberdeen for a joyful reunion with Leslie and the family. Over the following years, until Harry's death in 2009, the two families corresponded and met frequently with the bond that had kept the two men together during their fraught wartime service becoming closer over the passing years.

It had always saddened Leslie that the rest of the crew had lost contact with each other but Harry Brooker's friendship brought back many happy memories of their wartime service and it was through Harry's goodwill that Leslie was able to reassess his operational career. On learning that Leslie's logbook and diaries had sunk along with the drifter, Harry very kindly made all his records available to Leslie. The most important of these was his logbook and as the two men had flown all their 38 operations together it was easy to copy the details into a new logbook for Leslie and his family to treasure.

Now living in quiet retirement in his home in Canal Crescent, Port Elphinstone near Inverurie since Bess sadly passed away, Leslie is not only surrounded by his family and their families, he also has the cherished memories of his wartime exploits to look back on and savour. Mention the word '*Lancaster*' and his eyes light up in contemplative thought as he relives his nightly forays into the heart of Occupied Europe as a proud member of a Bomber Command squadron, a pride that has never, and quite rightly so, dimmed down the years.

In May 2011, work begins on a memorial to the 55,573 men lost whilst serving in Bomber Command. Made of Portland stone and designed by renowned architect Liam O'Connor, it will be erected in Green Park, Central London, and is scheduled for completion in May 2012. The roof of the pavilion will be open to the sky and the open entrance will be made from melted down aluminium from a crashed Halifax. Inside, sculptor Philip Jackson has created a bronze sculpture of a seven-man bomber crew which will commemorate those who died in the Halifax, OW-M of 426 Squadron, lost to a nightfighter on 12/13th May 1944. As well as a tribute to the dead of Bomber Command it is also a celebration of the service of those gallant men who survived. In the words of Lord Ashcroft, a respected historian and avowed collector of gallantry awards: *'Rarely, if ever, can any group of servicemen have been more deserving of a permanent memorial to their outstanding courage. Members of Bomber Command are truly worthy of their place in history among the bravest of the brave.'*

Let those words stand as a testament to Leslie Bruce Smith's service and courage also.

With the recent death of the last remaining World War One veteran Claude Choules in Australia, future generations will grow up without the benefit of his experiences of living history in their lifetime. So it will be with the World War Two veterans, as they gradually pass away another chapter in world history will close, leaving us with only their written and oral memories to paint a vivid picture of war. In Leslie's case, the tragedy is that so much of his written history sank with his belongings in 1951 on his ill-fated expedition. It is a shame that all of Leslie's documentation and photographs of his time with 61 Squadron didn't survive. By using the 97 Squadron mementoes which did survive, and his memories, we help preserve part of our country's history in this story as a reminder of the debt we owe to those who fought and all too often fell in our defence.

INNOCENCE.

How many nights, when just a boy, I'd lay curled up inside
my bed.
Listening to the thunderous roar, of engines.
Flying. Overhead.
And, running to the window
glimpsed the shadows of the
bomber's flight.
In all their metalled multitudes, death-laden fleets
that pierced the night.
Whose passing left me naught but pride,
a young boy's head filled with the lies.
Of men.
And politician's hate,
which sent our youth to darkened skies.
The fear and pain was theirs alone,
a parachute's silk white as
the shroud.
Where hunters stalked their prey on high,
stark silhouettes against the cloud.
The shattered town's crazed funeral pyres,
such nightmare sights
I never saw.
Nor cried as silent witness to,
the empty futileness of war.
Up, up aloft,
whilst young men fought, and died
and cursed,
and wept.
Far, far below. I slept.

Acknowledgements and Bibliography.

'Achieve Your Aim.' The History of 97 (Straits Settlement) Squadron in the Second World War. Kevin Bending. Woodfield Publishing 2005.
'Bomber Barons.' Chaz Bowyer.Published by William Kimber & Co Limited 1983.
'Britain at War' magazine. Published by Cabell Publishing Limited.
'German Night Fighter Force.' Gebhard Ebers. Jane's Publishing Company 1979.
'Lancaster Target.' Jack Currie. First published in 1977 by New English Library.
'Lancaster.' Leo McInstry. Published by John Murray (Publishers.) 2009.
'Lancaster. The Biography.' S/Leader Tony Iveson DFC. Published by Andre Deutsch 2009.
'No Moon Tonight.' Don Charlwood. Crecy Publishing 1994.
'The Bomber Command Diaries. An Operational Reference Book 1939-45.' Martin Middlebrook and Chris Everitt. First published by Viking 1985. Published by Penguin Books 1990.
'The Hardest Victory.' RAF Bomber Command in The Second World War. Denis Richards.
Published by Hodder and Stoughton 1994.
'The Right Of The Line.' The Royal Air Force In The European War 1939-45. John Terraine.
Published by Hodder and Stoughton 1985.
'Thundering Through The Clear Air.' No.61 (Lincoln Imp) Squadron at War. Derek Bramer.
Published TUCANN*designandprint* 1977.
'Withered Garland.' Group Captain Peter Johnson DSO OBE DFC AFC. Published by New European Publications Ltd 1995.

Online Resources.

www.lancaster-archive.com
www.97squadronassociation.co.uk
www.lostbombers.co.uk
www.raf.mod.uk/bombercommand
www.nationalarchives.gov.uk

Special Acknowledgements.

Special mention and thanks must go to Mr Kevin Bending whose dedication to the memory of 97 (Straits Settlement) Squadron has resulted in his remarkable website and book, without which much of this book would have remained unwritten.

To Derek Bramer as without his excellent history of 61 Sqn, *Thundering Through The Clear Air'* so much of that Sqn's wartime operational methods would have remained unknown.

Also to Martin Middlebrook and Chris Everitt whose *'The Bomber Command Diaries'* ISBN-0-14-012936-7 provides an unsurpassed reference starting point for anyone interested in the operational sorties of the RAF in World War Two.

The National Archives for their permission to use the Operational Logs of both 61 and 97 Sqn.

Grampian Police Archives for permission to use the images of the Aberdeen Blitz.

Mr Joe Sharp whose labour of love that is the online *'Lost bombers'* site enabled me to find so many details of a/c lost to both squadron's that would otherwise have been impossible.

CPSIA information can be obtained at www.ICGtesting.com
Printed in the USA
BVOW031032261011

274582BV00012B/32/P